The Courage To Say *"No More"*

The
Courage
To Say
"No More"

Reclaiming Your Life After
Emotional Abuse

Second Edition

Tracy Kemble, Ph.D.

Contents

Introduction

"There have been a lot of "Nevers" in my life. For example, at one time I told myself I would never get divorced, never be depressed, and certainly, I would never be suicidal. Then my life changed, and I thought I would never be free from fear, never be happy, and never be able to forgive. I guess this book could have been called, "Never Say Never." Instead, I called it "The Courage to Say, "No More."
Welcome to the Second Round of *Courage*

My name is Tracy Kemble. Over twenty years ago, I wrote those opening words in the first edition of my best seller book, ***The Courage to Say "No More!"***

Since the original release of this book, I'm told those words have impacted readers from around the globe. My followers have shared that the healing message of "**Courage**" has reached from the Americas into Asia and Europe. It has ventured into South Africa and South America. It has made its way down under to Australia. And **"Courage"** has even made its impact in parts of the Middle East. Hillary Clinton recognized this work as "an excellent role model for healing." And for women coming out of abuse, "Courage" has been referred to as the "Bible of recovery" for many during their initial steps of healing. *Never*, would I have imagined my story about recovery would have impacted so many.

The New Courage

On the twenty-year anniversary of this landmark book, I felt it was time to write a second edition of **The Courage to Say "No More."** I say that because since the original release of **Courage**, much has changed.

To start, when I first wrote "**Courage**" I was simply an "everyday" woman; meaning I was just "Tracy," a young American female who after surviving years of mental abuse, found my first voice, my *courage*, and most exciting, my personal path to healing. My initial message was simple, but as a newly healed abuse survivor, I didn't mind. I was passionate about my recovery, and at the time, my dream was to take what little knowledge I had and share it with others in need; which I did.

Twenty years later however, as I venture into **The Courage to Say "No More" 2.0,** both my personal and professional knowledge about abuse, and more importantly, about the *recovery* of abuse. has significantly expanded.

For example, today I am a Ph.D. whose awareness has expanded from innocently believing that abuse was a isolated, private "family matter", to understanding that abuse is a global issue affecting 1 in 3 women around the world (UN Women, Facts and Figures: Ending Violence Against Women, February 2016).

Today I am the founder of The W.I.N. Foundation®, which is a 501-C3 non-profit organization that specializes in Abuse Recovery (www.WINFoundationInternational.org). I am a mentor who has helped over 175,000 women heal from the pains of abuse. And as a front-line teacher and educator, I am a featured guest lecturer for police, pastoral, professional, and media around the world.

Over the years, my involvement in the world of recovery has ranged from holding the hand of a scared victim in an Emergency Room, all the way to assisting governments construct laws for the protection of women. This edition of *The Courage to Say, "No More!"* reflects that experience, and in Part IV, *The Ten Steps to Healing,* I have imparted new methods of recovery that were not available at the original writing of this book.

Another shift in *The Courage to Say, "No More!" 2.0* is the exclusion of religious references. I made this change because over the past two decades, not only have I expanded into new understandings of spirituality myself, but more important I have discovered that without a doubt, abuse is a global issue. Meaning, every country, culture, *and every religion* in the world faces its traumas. My front row seat has validated that abuse, unfortunately, *has no prejudices.* It is a condition that affects both the God-fearing and non-god fearing, including Christians, Muslims, Hindus, Catholics, Jewish and any other religious group that believes or does *not* believe in a Higher Power. Therefore, this edition of *"The Courage to Say "No More!"* does not have religious affiliations. God, Allah, The Divine, Spirit, or however you define your Higher Power is a personal choice. My job via the message of this book, is simply to share healing.

What Remains the Same

When reconstructing the second edition of" *The Courage to Say "No More!"* I felt it was important to keep my organic, unedited journal-based voice.

I must admit, I struggled with this decision because who I am today, is not who I once was. I felt though, it was necessary to leave the person I was during the abuse, *intact*; not only to appreciate how healing has changed me, but more so, to make sure that others in pain know they're not alone in their insanity.

As You Begin

As you begin your journey into *The Courage to Say "No More!"* I want to emphasize as I did in the first previous edition that this book is not about criticizing or placing blame. Nor is it a book about self-pity, or about self-proclamation. Instead, *The Courage to Say, "No More!"* is a book about surviving and learning to start over. It's a book about self-responsibility and self-respect. It's a book about growing, forgiving, overcoming and healing. Most of all however, it's a book about *loving*. Meaning, it's a book about learning the importance of loving yourself first, then loving others in healthy ways, when the time is right.

There was a time in my life when sharing my vulnerabilities would have embarrassed me. Twenty years later however, as I re-release **The Courage to Say, "No More!"** it is my *privilege* to share my deepest thoughts for those in need. It is my *joy* to help others learn from my experiences and insights. And it's my *responsibility* to share my message that says, no matter what type of abuse you are facing, healing and happiness are possible, as long as you gain the *courage* to pursue them.

I will once again start this book with a word of wisdom my mother taught me while I was on my road to recovery. She once said, "You only have two choices when it comes to hard times. You can lie down and die to them, or you can stand-up and meet your challenge."

The Courage to Say, "No More!" is about learning to stand-up and meet your challenge. My hope, as you read my story, is that you too will find your courage, your healing, and most important the Self-Love you need to heal your heart, mind and soul from the pains of abuse.

It took me over a year and a half to finish this new version of "Courage"; which was about a year longer than I had anticipated. Therefore, with no more words needed, and *a lot* of path to cover, after twenty years and six months in the making, it is with love, honor and respect, I gift you **The Courage to Say, "No More!"**, 2nd *edition*.

Because Self Love is Non-Negotiable

Dr. Tracy Kemble

DISCLAIMER

Some of the names in this book were changed for protection. Language and content may be considered violent and offensive. No parts of this book are intended as a substitute for diagnosis or treatment of any condition. The content is for informational use only.

Part I

My Journal

1

My Journal

Journal Entry December 17 (year 3 in the abuse)

"...Does he love me? Or does he hate me? My answer is unknown. On one hand, he loves no other greater than me; yet at the same time hates no other greater than me, either. It's as though I am his greatest joy and his greatest pain; his brightest angel and his darkest demon, all in one. I am the woman he hates to love and worse, I am the woman he loves to hate... the pain is unbearable..."

Journal Entry May 2 (year 4 in the abuse)

*"...The fear that I feel when I see him,
it makes my blood run cold.
The fear that I feel when I hear him,
it makes my heart feel old.
I prepare myself for his worst,
 yet I pray for his best.
Oh God... which will it be today..."*

Journal Entry February 12 (year 5 in the abuse)

"... I was once the color of many rainbows, the fragrance of blooming flowers, the taste of many wines. But now I am none of these. Now, my rainbow has turned to gray; my fragrances have lost their scent, and my wines have soured with forgotten time. I am lifeless and colorless. I am tasteless and forgotten. How sad life becomes when hope is deferred..."

Journal Entry March 27 (year 5 in the abuse)

"He says a kind word, I throw him a party. He performs a kind act, I throw him a parade. What the mind of an emotionally bankrupt person will celebrate.

Perhaps his kind actions are normal to some, even expected by others. But to a person who is like sun-dried clay, I welcome even the slightest drop of moisture that comes my way..."

Journal Entry April 6 (year 5 in the abuse)

"...His anger is like a Jack in the Box... an unwanted attack waiting to happen. Its wrath lurks beneath his hardened face... waiting...waiting... waiting to rears its ugly head at the slightest wrong twist of life. Why must I be that wrong twist of life? Why must I be the one he attacks without warning - making my heart freeze in fear and making my blood run cold..."

Journal Entry April 10 (year 5 in the abuse)

"...It's a radical roller coaster ride some call love. No one intentionally gets on; but once you are, it becomes an addictive drug that's life-giving and life-taking all in one. Its highs don't compare to anything you've experienced. Its lows run so deep, no blackness can describe. It makes you feel alive and dead... pumped-up and persecuted, all in one. It's the Hellish roller coaster ride called Love..."

Journal Entry March 17 (year 5 in the abuse)

"...My mind is slowly slipping away from me and I have begun to accept the unthinkable. It's as though I have drunk the poison of denial and I sit in a chamber, deep within myself. I see what is happening and yet... the voice within me no longer cries out for it to stop. Is it too weak? Or is it too scared? Or has it simply lost the will to fight?"

Journal Entry September 5 (year 5 in the abuse)

"...To the outside world, it sounds crazy, but to me it sounds so logical: **All** *I do, I do for love. I stay because I fear losing love, believing that if I love harder, the fear will end. Yet in the end I'm consumed with fear anyway. Why? Because I have lost love... that is the love for ME. It is gone, just like a faint thought in a distant dream... something I once knew existed, but now I cannot quite remember. And because of this, it's as though fear and love are now one and the same. I guess that is why I stay... Now it all feels like love to me..."*

Journal Entry May 8 (year 7)

"...I think that time heals most wounds, as it makes you forget certain things: Like, I cannot remember the smell of his skin or even the tone of his voice anymore. But then again maybe healing happens from trying not to remember..."

Journal Entry December 21 (year 8)

"I never knew if my story needed to be told. But this afternoon a group of children were teasing each other in the courtyard outside my house.

Their playtime went from a game of laughter and fun to a violent exchange of nasty insults.

Finally, when the last verbal punch was thrown I heard a small voice say, "Sticks and stones may break my bones, but words will never harm me!"

As a young child, I remember believing that "words could never harm me." But as a young woman, I have learned differently. I've learned that sticks and stones can break your bones, but I've also learned that words can do just as much trauma and damage. I have learned that words, if thrown often enough, can lodge themselves in your mind and come back to haunt you when no one else is around. I've learned that words if thrown hard enough can break your spirit. And I've learned that words, if thrown creatively and manipulatively enough, can make you believe in lies.

It is true that sticks and stones can break your bones. But it is not true that words will never harm you. Words can cause the final blow that will kill your self-esteem."

Part II

The Beginning of The End

2

The Beginning of the End

Journal Entry - February 10 (year 9)

"Nobody told me about it.
The warning signs, the effects, the pain.
Nobody told me about it
The damage, the fear, the shame.

Nobody told me if left untreated,
it only proceeds to get worse.
Nobody told me the scars it leaves
makes life so painful on earth.

Nobody told me about
how it could happen to me.
If only they told me about it,
how different my life might be...

Oh God, may I never be too ashamed to tell my story."

I am sitting in Maui, Hawaii. It is 5:30 in the morning and I am peacefully watching the sunrise from my bed. I take a moment and breath in the orange palette of light, and think to myself how the Universe is showing off to me again.

Spyro, my newlywed husband, sleeps peacefully next to me.

Then, as though he senses I'm watching him, he opens his sparkling blue eyes and says his ritual morning "Hellos."

"Good morning Love of My Life, you are so beautiful..." I smile and gently touch his arm at his kind words.

The sight from our hotel room is incredible this morning: The majestic blue sea lapping in the distance, the palm trees swaying in the trade winds, the brilliant Hawaiian sun making its grand entrance onto this side of the world. The sight is magnificent. But then again, my *life* is magnificent. The past six months have been a *magical* whirlwind for me: Getting married; winning Mrs. Globe; traveling to six countries in six months; hosting international telecasts, being the guest of Presidents. My goodness, how different my life is today, compared to only a few short years ago...

Journal Entry - March 5 (year 4 in the abuse)

"It is 4:00 am and I don't know where my husband is. I've called the Highway Patrol, but they have no reports of any accidents. I've called the hospitals, but they have no record of his name. Is he okay? Is he dead? Is he out with another woman? Oh my God, did he go to Vegas again? Oh no... please NO!

I feel like I'm going crazy, God. I feel like I'm losing my grip, as the more I try to make things better, the worst things seem to get!"

Some might wonder *how* a person reaches such crazy states of existence. Trust me when I say, I've challenged myself with that question at least *nine million times* over the years. Today however, when I reflect on my journey into the insanity of abuse, with self-great compassion and clarity, it is *easy* to share the "why" behind my pain.

Journal Entry - October 4 (Ground Zero)
"...I started my new job this week. I met so many interesting people, including a guy who claims I will be his wife! He seemed humored and yet, angry when I told him that I wasn't on the menu."

Journal Entry - October 23 (week 3)
"This guy is interesting to me; mysterious in a strange way. He studies every move I make. He listens to every word I say. He, distantly yet precisely watches over me; much like a hawk watches his obvious prey."

Journal Entry - December 1 (month 3)
"I'm not quite sure what to make of him... I have turned him down three times for a date, but he says he won't take 'no' for an answer. Yesterday he sent flowers to my grandmother. (I wonder how he found out where she lives?) Tonight, he gave my mother flowers when she came to see me at work. Earlier today, he covered my car with flowers while I was in school, and when I say covered, I mean covered! For whatever reason, he is most definitely determined to get my attention."

Ground Zero

I met him in the fall of my senior year in college. It was the first day of my new job, and from the start he said I was *the one* for him. In hindsight, two opposites souls should've never met.

I was a naive 22-year-old. An overly-sheltered, "born-again" Christian, who lacked real-life experience, and who believed *anything* could be solved with a pageant smile and a prayer.

He on the other hand, was the tough-skinned quiet type. A stone-faced American-Irishman, who lived behind a wall, who rarely smiled, and whose eyes had stories no soul should know.

I was innocent. He was worldly. I was a college graduate. He barely finished high school. *I was the challenge and he was the attention-giver.* Together, we were the toxic two-some and when our chemistries mixed, we poisoned each other's lives.

It took only a few weeks before we started dating and shortly into our relationship, he shared his tragic upbringing with me. He told me stories about a father who drank too much and spent time in jail; about a mother, who, to feed her six children, went on food stamps to survive; and about a family who took him into bankruptcy at the young age of 24. He told me how he grew up quick; how his family lived on the run because of his father's continuous bouts with the law; and how, due to the constant childhood upheavals, he never had the chance to *be* a child. He shared how he never participated in team sports; how he never learned to sing, dance or play an instrument; and how he never took part in a school play or group project. With a stone-like delivery, he also proudly shard that he *never* once shed a tear over his childhood voids.

The Sullivan Family

It was Christmas Eve when I met his family for the first time, and when I arrived at their house, I thought I was at the wrong place.

You see, based on the stories, I expected to see a rundown house in a rundown neighborhood; an indigent-like family who drove old cars, and wore secondhand clothes. I expected to see a mother who was on her last leg, and an unshaven, unkempt, whisky-reeking father, with a brown paper sack in one hand and smoldering cigarette from the other. I expected to see a smoke-filled shambled house with dirty, untamed kids, and an overgrown front yard that screamed of extreme neglect. But when I arrived that Christmas Eve and met "the" family for the first time, what I expected was *not* what I saw at all.

Much to my surprise, when I pulled my car into the driveway, I arrived at a house that looked more like a holiday window at Harrods Department Store, than like a *brand-new* track home. There were red Christmas lights and holiday décor *everywhere*; and when I say everywhere, I mean they were *every*where: Santa and his reindeer adorned the chimney, red bulbs wrapped the windows like life-size presents, a Winter Wonderland covered the front lawn, and even the doorbell chimed a Christmas tune when pressed.

Much to my surprise, that evening I also met a family that was much *different* than I expected; *a lot* different than described, as the family I met that night *affectionately* teased each other and laughed *a lot*. They seemed to authentically protect one another. And for sure by all first impressions, they genuinely appeared to love each other.

I must confess, my first impression of Erik's family was not anything what I expected. I didn't expect to see a brand-new home accented with *two* brand-new cars in the driveway. I didn't expect to meet a polite and warm family that welcomed me with laughter into their festive home. I didn't expect to meet a darling mother who was draped in diamond rings and designer clothes. And most of all, I didn't expect the show-quality, ceiling-high Christmas that was brilliantly lit with hundreds of bulbs, whose cap lightly brushed against the 20-foot high vaulted ceiling, and whose base was *literally* surrounded in dozens, upon dozens, upon *dozens* of gifts, toys, and presents. As God as my witness, there was literally no space to walk in the largest room of the house because underneath the steroid-sized tree, the carpet literally was blanketed from end-to-end in holiday exchange.

They say that hindsight is always 20/20 and in "hindsight" I must agree, as when I look back on my introduction to Erik's family, I can clearly say that meeting The Sullivans for that first time was not *anything* near what I had expected. Five and a half years later though, I my hindsight would tell me that that first impressions are *not* always what they seem.

3

The Family

MEMO FROM NORMAL LAND®

"If you want to know what type of fruit you are eating,

look at the tree from which it dropped."

Erik

Journal Entry - October 7 (year 7)

"...If only I knew then what I know now, how different my life would be; how different my love would be; how different my choices would be."

His name was Erik. He was the second in line of six children and out of the entire Sullivan clan, he was the one who laughed the least, and worried the most. Oddly, he was the hero of the family and believe it or not, the sanest one of the group. I remember one time a friend of his once told me, "It's amazing he turned out as he did, *considering* his family of origin." I understood later what she meant.

Erik was a handsome man; tall, and lean, and stood over 6'2." He had fair Irish skin, thinning brown hair and distant, trauma-washed eyes. He was an impeccable dresser; extremely organized; and most undeniable to everyone, Erik was a *bonafide* Perfectionist.

He was by no means an approachable man. In fact, his character could best be described as a bullheaded, pride-filled man, who *no one,* including the law, his employers and especially his wife, was *ever* to tell him what to do.

He called it the "No Comment" Rule, and it applied to all areas of his life, including his home, his work, and especially for some reason, his driving; where Erik was what I called a *calculated* reckless driver.

I say that because one of Erik's "forms of entertainment" (as he would say) was taking people on reckless joyrides. For whatever reason, Erik loved getting a rise (or a scream or even a tear) out of his powerless passengers; especially for some reason, when that passenger was me.

On too many occasions, just for kicks Erik would recklessly drive around our neighborhood and threaten to flip the car with me in it. The traumatizing Hell ride wouldn't stop until I was begging and crying for him to let me out of the car; which of course, he never did. I'll never know why Erik enjoyed seeing me in such a state-of-terror. But for whatever reason, the sight of me shaking and crying always made him laugh with joy.

Erik was an angry and violent young man and more often than not, his temper got him into trouble. Especially when paired with his favorite beverage of choice, *Jack Daniels on the rocks.* Over the years, I heard countless bar-brawl stories bookended with *Jack Daniels* on one side, and emergency ambulance rides *for his victims* on the other.

Erik claimed he never remembered his brawls or beatings. He said when he "went nuts" on his victims (as he would describe it) he would slip into another world; a "black-out zone", he would say. Then, once there, he would beat *and beat* on his victim until someone pulled him off the poor bleeding soul.

Erik shared that only once he recalled coming out of his "nuts zone" on his own. It was the time the blood from the man whose head he was slamming into a car windshield splattered him on the face. Erik hated blood, and the feeling of the warm fluid splashing against his own skin was more intense than his bashing a man's head against a car window.

I asked Erik once if he would ever hit a woman. He told me, "Only if she hits me first." It was statement that to this day I will never forget.

Erik was a religious, not a spiritual man and I never figured out if he practiced Catholicism to appease his mother, or to satisfy himself. To Erik, Mass was his trump card to "sin" as he would say – not to mention his *excuse* to get "the slut" (as he called *any* woman who slept with him) out of his bed by morning. For whatever reason, Erik *never* allowed a woman to stay overnight with him. He considered *that* "too ungodly."

Erik had a few close friends who called themselves "The Wrecking Crew." I always enjoyed the times *The Crew* came around because they made Erik laugh; and seeing Erik laugh was *important* to me. Outside of the Wrecking Crew moments, Erik didn't laugh much. Except that was, when he was laughing at someone else, or laughing at me.

That however was the norm for Erik. His humor was cutting and cruel and the rule of thumb was that he could poke fun at you, but you never dared poke back at him. If you did, there was too hefty of a price to pay for bumping into his fragile self-esteem.

In hindsight, I won't go as far to say that Erik was a bad man. I think it is safer to say that unfortunately he was the son of an alcoholic. He was a victim of *traumatic* childhood abuse. Yet up until the day I left, he was never able to recognize that.

Margaret

Journal Entry (year 3 in the abuse)

"... Her laugh is interesting to me. It's as though behind every light chuckle, there is a painful tear dying to be heard..."

Margaret, Erik's mother, was a fanatic about three things: Being a good Catholic, being thin and having a clean house. She was overly naive for a woman her age and oddly, she was obsessed with being a "Good Girl."

Margaret didn't work outside of the home and oddly enough, even with her beautiful personality, she didn't have any real friends. Unfortunately, any friends she did make were always lost every time the family had to up-and-move to avoid her husband's bout with the law.

Erik greatly feared for the well-being of his mother, and being the family hero that he was, he tried his best to provide a false sense of protection - *by giving her credit cards for "just in case" purposes.* Needless to say, "just in case" happened a lot with Margaret during our marriage.

Catholicism was the foundation of Margaret's life and for a short time, she taught Catechism classes at her local church. It was her dream to teach for the Church, but sadly soon after her first session, her husband made her quit. He said she was becoming "a bad wife" from all the time she spent away from home. To keep the peace, Margaret stopped teaching Catechism, and when she did, something in her died. But of course, it did. A person is *never* to abandon their dreams or passions for someone else.

Outside of her husband and children, Margaret didn't connect with her extended family. Her sister and mother were alive, but they never came to see her. On the flip side, she also never went to see them. She claimed she didn't take trips to see her family because she was too afraid to leave her husband alone. The chains of co-dependence are truly crippling.

To Margaret, her children were her *everything*. In fact, happiness for her would have been to have all her children living in the same house with her until she died.

She *almost* succeeded in making that happen, as the year before I left, she had all but two children *and their families* living with her.

Of the two that lived "off-property", one was only 20 minutes from her home. As for the other? He and I were on the opposite side of the country; yet without my knowledge, Erik had requested a job transfer where he identified Florida (the hometown of his family) as his relocation destination.

I always wondered if Margaret's goal to have her adult children live with her was motivated by her desire to be in control? Or was it driven by her need to feel protected from the insanity of her husband's alcoholism? I guess I will never know.

There is no doubt that Margaret was a pure soul. She was a devout Catholic who went to Mass every day, never touched alcohol and most impressively, considering her household, she *never* used foul language.

I asked Erik once if his mother *ever* swore or sipped on wine. He told me she did order a glass in a restaurant *once*, but her drunk husband publicly humiliated her for it. Apparently, after she took the first sip he started yelling in front of on-lookers that she "had no class" for drinking wine in public. Erik said after that, she never touched alcohol again.

When I first met Margaret, I remember her laughing a lot. However, I barely remember her laughing near the end of our relationship. In fact, I only remember her crying, a lot.

The last time I saw dear Margaret she barely weighed 100 pounds, had slipped into a deep depression and only left her bedroom once in a blue moon. The sad part was that no one did anything to help. They just let her slip away.

John Senior

Journal Entry (year 2 in the abuse)

"...There is something about him that frightens me. He's like a frustrated prisoner captured in the craziness of his mind. He however, doesn't care... To him, it's more fun to stay in the secrets and the chaos of his dark side..."

John Sr. was the father of Erik. He was a Brooklyn-born, New York Irishman. He was the son an alcoholic, a heavy filter-less cigarette smoker, and most noticeably, he was a person who trusted no one, not even himself.

John Sr. had a tongue like a machete and without a second thought he could slice you up and spit you out in a single sentence; which is what he did to everyone in his family, except to me. For some reason, he never did it to me.

John Sr. was a violent man, both physically and verbally. And over the years Erik would tell me countless stories about a childhood filled with his father's temper and terror.

I would hear stories about a family who hid behind locked doors to avoid beatings from John Sr.; about how he and his older brother would pray to God that their drunkard father would pass out before he could make it up the stairs to "get them." And I would hear about the secrets they were *forced* to keep and about the violence that happened behind their closed doors. The saddest thing is that Erik considered this all "normal."

John Sr., (like Margaret) also had no real friends in his life. And like Margaret he too did not speak to his family. I met his brothers only once at our wedding. But following the *bloody* event, they swore never to return. True to their word, they never did.

John Sr. was a writer and a criminal, the author of an unpublished story about his life and the mastermind behind an insurance fraud against his newspaper company that sent him to prison. After his time behind bars, he never worked a legitimate job again. Erik told me countless times that prison took something out of his dad. Including apparently, his desire to work or provide for his family.

After his prison term John Sr. "supported" his family off his questionable lawsuits *and his children's credit cards.* Once, in an act of generosity, he opened a credit card in Erik's name and distributed a *complimentary* card to every member of the family who was old enough to use it. And use it they did, to the tune of $30,000 of credit card debt in two months. No one ever apologized for the credit card abuse. Nor did they think twice about repaying the debt.

John Sr. was a fugitive from the law. He was an alcoholic and a crack user; and the strangest thing is that somehow, he was likable and detestable all at the same time. In hindsight, I believe his family spent a lifetime trying to keep him sober and straight. And in hindsight, I think he both loved and hated them for trying.

David

Journal Entry (year 2 in the abuse)

".. Are eyes truly the window to the soul? If so, his angry infused eyes tell stories that no man should hear..."

David was the oldest brother in the Sullivan clan, and when

he came around, everyone seemed to feel a little safer. He made the "money" in the family and like all the Sullivan adult children, he too felt obligated to share most of it with the entire group.

David was a good-looking Irishman; a charismatic business executive with a smile that could electrify a room. He loved women, toys, booze and horses, and he played hard with all of them, even after he was married.

He married a girl named Tammy, and poor Tammy. The Sullivan family despised her, as well as her two young children from her previous marriage.

There's no question that Tammy was a bit rough around the edges. She was a former stripper and also a survivor of abuse. On the surface, we had nothing in common - *except* that we shared the bond of being with men that were married to their families instead of to us.

The entire family, especially John Sr., was cruel and abusive to Tammy and her two young children. In fact, not a single gathering could pass without her getting one of John Sr.'s horrible tongue lashings.

He typically only beat on Tammy verbally. But one night during a drunken stupor, he got *so* enraged with her that he started throwing pool balls at her head. She had to run out of the house with one child in each hand to avoid getting injured.

Tammy took a lot of abuse from John Sr. over the years and oddly enough, David never stopped him. Occasionally when things got dreadfully wrong she would take her children and leave. But more often than not she stayed and tolerated it.

Tammy was somewhat protected from John Senior's bashings. But that changed when a year before I left, the police were again moving in on John Sr., and David moved his parents, his younger sister, Desiree, her husband, their baby, and his two youngest siblings to Florida. John Sr. was supposed to serve a jail sentence for a drunk-driving violation. He left town though, and moved to Florida to avoid serving time. David, in turn, bought them a ranch style house on the shores of Mandarin Bay, put luxury cars in their garage, and financed their life off his company credit cards.

The last I heard of David was that he ended up bankrupt and jobless. I guess he jeopardized everything for his parents. Or should I say, for *The Family*.

Desiree

Journal Entry (year 3 in the abuse)

> *"...This is a life that is screaming out for help. The only problem is that her screams are killing me in the process..."*

Desiree was the next sibling in the Sullivan clan. She was the oldest of Erik's three younger sisters, and she and I were the same age.

Desiree had a great sense of humor, and an impeccable taste in clothes. But she was a drama junkie, and everyone in the family bought into the production, except for *me*.

During the time I knew Desiree she got into three car accidents, had a tubule pregnancy, fell down a flight of stairs, had fainting spells, black-out headaches, eating disorders, stomach disorders, prescription addictions as well as numerous miscarriages without DNC's. In fact, her *drama addiction* was so intense that not a single event could pass without an award-winning performance, including the night she had her first baby.

I'll never forget that night. It was 2:00 in the morning and suddenly Erik yanked me out of bed. Margaret was on the phone informing us that Desiree, who was in labor, had requested to see a priest for her last rites. Desiree thought she was dying. Erik, in turn hung-up the phone, demanded that I get on my knees and pray because "Desiree was going to die."

I shook my head in my sleep-deprived state and told Erik that Desiree was *not dying.* Desiree was *giving birth,* and I would pray for the epidural to quickly take effect. In hindsight, I guess everyone screams for help their own way. Drama was Desiree's drug of choice.

While growing up, Desiree looked to Erik as her protector, and I must say that he did a good job. Erik was the one who kept her safe, and who had the final approval or *disapproval* of her boyfriends; which over the years he disapproved of all, but one. Desiree's favorite story to share was about how Erik would wait in the entryway of their house when she was on a date. The moment Erik heard the car, he would race outside pull her out of the vehicle, and send the young man on his way.

For whatever reason, Erik was overly obsessed with his sister's virginity, and on the flip side, Desiree was obsessed with having Erik protect her. For years the two played off of each other - her dramatizing the role of the damsel-in-distress and he playing the role of the mighty protector. Many young men who crossed her path were sadly beaten to a pulp upon her cry for help.

When David or Erik wasn't around, Desiree then became the parent of the clan; financing the family household, and making sure to meet everyone's needs. Erik felt bad for Desiree when she had to take the burden of being the "family protector." That's why he too gave her a credit card for "just in case" purposes. Needless to say, *"just in case"* also happened *a lot* with Desiree during our marriage.

Desiree was the 4-1-1 in the family. She would tell me countless stories of how her father had his ex-partner in the newspaper business killed after he turned state evidence against

John Sr., in the insurance fraud. She shared how he was part of the Irish Mafia; how he molested her, and how he consistently cheated on her mother. She told me about the gun-carrying drug dealers who came knocking down her door demanding money that John Sr. owed them from one of his many crack sprees. And she was also the one who told me that one of David's ex-girlfriends ended up in a psych ward after their relationship. At first, I thought it was due to the trauma *of* the breakup. But I would eventually learn it was the *drama* of the family that sent her over the edge.

Holly

> ***Journal Entry (year 3 in the abuse)***
>
> *"...It amazes me that she can laugh so easily, even with all the craziness. Perhaps she is more protected than the rest of us. Or perhaps her laughter is just a shield to hide the pain..."*

Holly was next in line, and I loved her a lot because she had this amazing ability to find laughter in most everything. Time would show however that underneath her bursts of joy brewed a wicked temper that when ignited, burned anything that dared stand in its path.

Holly and I became close near the end of my relationship with Erik because we started talking about the craziness in the family. She recognized it after she, her husband and their two children moved *back* to California from Florida.

Initially, they moved to Florida to get a new start. Holly and her husband Doug had a hard time on a bartender's salary with four mouths to feed. They were financially sinking in California and every month they took money from John Sr. and Margaret to survive. But when John Sr. and Margaret couldn't afford to give, which was more often than not, the burden would fall on David, Erik and me. Finally, after months of begging by Margaret, and promises of a corporate job by David, they packed their van and moved across the country to Florida.

Unfortunately, the months that followed though proved to be nothing they expected. Doug didn't get the corporate job he was promised by David, and found himself *again* working late nights earning a bartender's salary. To make matters worse, John Sr. and Margaret insisted that Doug's paychecks go into *their* account since Doug and Holly were living with them.

That proved to be a disaster because when school started, Margaret took the money and bought *her* two youngest children school clothes; even though Holly's babies didn't have coats for the winter.

In many ways, I felt sorry for Holly and Doug. They had a hard life from the start of their relationship. Doug had big plans on making it in the entertainment business, but those came crashing down when Holly became pregnant "out of wedlock." The family, especially Margaret, was distraught when she heard the news. She loathed the idea that the couple was having sex outside of marriage; *almost more than John Senior loathed Doug himself.*

Poor Doug. As a family outsider, he too took a lot of Sullivan bashing over the years. Yet In spite of the abuse, he truly loved Holly and married her after the baby was born in a Las Vegas ceremony.

I didn't go to the Las Vegas wedding. And I am glad. Like most family encounters, it too ended in a bloody street brawl. Apparently while waiting at an intersection on Las Vegas Boulevard, Desiree had one of her damsel attacks. She claimed the young man standing next to her at the light said something derogatory. In response, she screamed, threw a Coke in his face and Erik, being the family protector began beating the daylights out of the stranger; all the while both Desiree's and Holly's husbands stood back and watched. Erik and Desiree always laughed when they collectively shared that story. I always got sick to my stomach when I heard it.

Before I left The Sullivan's for good, Holly started having flashbacks of David molesting her. I asked her if she ever sought help for the trauma, and she told me that once she tried to tell her parents about what had happened. But no one believed her, so she never mentioned it again.

Holly abruptly left Florida and returned to California after David took her oldest daughter without permission. The flashback memories of what could happen were more than she could handle.

Like all the younger siblings, Holly also viewed Erik as a fatherly protector. And I have to say, he did a good job. When Holly was five years old, one night a drunkard John Sr. held a knife to her little face during dinner. Erik being the good protector frantically grabbed Holly from her chair, and the four of them ran out of the house for safety.

Holly remembers walking down the street, holding onto the hand of one of her older siblings and crying hysterically. They apparently sought shelter at a neighbor's house. But *two* whole days passed before Margaret retrieved her children.

I remember listening with amazement when Holly shared this story. How could Margaret allow this to happen? How could she let her husband wave a knife in her daughter's little face? How could she allow two days to pass before caring for her scared babies? And how could she let someone treat *her* so poorly?

I have to admit that at that time, I didn't understand the effects of abuse, and rather than listen with compassion, I instead judged Margaret and her reckless behavior. Then I vowed would I *never* allow something like that to happen to me, or to my future children. I guess that is where the old term, "Never Say 'Never' was formed.

Nicole & Little John

Journal Entry (year 3 in the abuse)

"...They think that they are keeping secrets, but these children are not stupid. Can't anyone hear the stress behind the grinding of her teeth? Can't they see the rage behind his young rebellious actions? Doesn't anybody care what this world of craziness is doing to the minds of these children? Oh God, I fear for their future. Oh God, I fear for their lives..."

Nicole and Little John were the youngest of the group. I met them when they were still in elementary school and the best way I can describe them is to say that there were innocent, yet worldly at the same time.

Nicole, like Holly, smiled all the time. She loved to laugh, she loved to perform, and most definitely, she loved her older brother, Erik.

Like most addictions, the adults in the family thought they were keeping the secrets of alcoholism away from the "little kids." But that was not the case. Nicole suffered from consistent nightmares, and when the visions that haunted her sleep didn't wake her, she would grind her teeth so loudly that you could hear it from the hallway.

As for Little John, who was the youngest of the clan, he also *deeply* loved his older brother, Erik. And Erik authentically tried to be a good influence on him. It worked for a while, but when the family unexpectedly moved to Florida, things changed. Little John began getting expelled from Junior High, primarily for fist fights and arguments.

The last time I saw Little John I asked him what he wanted to be when he grew up. He told me, "I want to be just like my dad; a rich man who never has to work." Deception is a nasty example.

My time with the Sullivans was around five and a half years in total. Over that period, I discovered that behind the mask of love and devotion the Sullivans portrayed, was the destructive and deadly disease of alcoholism - a disease that destroyed, manipulated and controlled their lives for years, and as a result, it was a progressive illness that changed my life forever.

4

The First Mistake

I should never have entered into a relationship when I first met Erik. That's because *emotionally* speaking, I was in *no* place to *be* in a relationship. You, however, would have *never* known.

On the *outside* (Pageant Smile girl that I was) I appeared to be fine. In fact, I seemed to be great.

I had recently finished my university studies. I got my first *paying* broadcast journalism job, which *I loved*. I was newly single. I was winning pageants, traveling a bit, and *externally* speaking, the world was at my feet.

On the *inside,* however, things were not as sparkling. On the inside, I was emotionally bankrupt, bottomed-out, and like the famous Jackson Browne song says, "I was running on empty."

One could say I had a lot *changes* in my life before meeting Erik. Changes that included my 17-year-old younger sister being locked down in a center for substance abuse (stuff like that *always* unpacks a lot of hidden family pain). Changes like, getting cold feet and canceling my engagement to my minister fiancée (which even though it was good for me, it was a *difficult* choice, none-the-less). And did I mention the unexpected divorce of my parents after 25 years of marriage?

That one, to say the least, I never saw coming, but when it hit, it ripped the foundation beneath me and sent me falling. Falling that is, right in a relationship where I convinced myself that if I absorbed my focus in someone else's pain, I would *not* have to face the blaring miseries of my own.

My Spiral into Hell

Many people wonder how things get so out of control in abusive relationships. Or, they question *how* things reach such crazy levels of insanity. The only way I can answer that question is to say, "It happens very slowly."

The best correlation to describe *how* the spiral into abuse happens is to compare it to music. In music, one instrument or layer of sound is placed on the next, and at some point, that single note turns into a multi-layered masterpiece of sound.

In the case of abuse, it works much the same way. Abuse also happens *layer by layer*. However, instead of the layers creating a beautiful masterpiece of sound, they instead create a masterpiece of manipulation that over time, kills, steals and destroys the life on the receiving end.

My First Layer of Abuse

In hindsight, the first note or the first layer of abuse with Erik all started with a curt correction. It came in the package of an unsolicited piece of "corrective advice" that he gave "in my best interest"; and under the guise of love, care, and concern.

In a short matter of time, his curt corrections (which established a norm) *slowly* merged into *non-verbal public* warning stares. Stares that he directed at me with laser precision whenever he didn't approve of something I said or did *in public.* Which in hindsight, started to happen more often.

The *non-verbal* public warning stares then *slowly* progressed into what I call *private, mini-*scolding or *mini-*lectures. These *private* lectures happened *after* I did something Erik did not approve of in public.

I always knew when I committed one of the "non approved" actions because the moment we left our public place, a long *silent* car ride home would ensure. Then after he felt his silence was punishing enough, he would finally present my list of horrific "public inappropriateness" that was then followed by a reprimanding hour-long lecture about my need for change.

When I look back on my gateway into abuse, I clearly see the one grave mistake I made with Erik: From the beginning of our relationship, I never held him *accountable* for his actions.

Meaning, from the start I made *excuses* for his bad behavior whenever he acted controlling or abusive. In other words, I never held him *accountable* when he would misbehave. I did instead what many women empathic women do, which was make excuses for Erik's abuse. Excuses like "he had a bad day," "a bad week" or even "a bad life."

From day one, I *never* held Erik responsible for his actions. I never, as both the Bible and Buddha say, let him "reap what he would sow." Instead, Erik would plant stones of inappropriateness, and I out of "love" (or what I would later discover was Love Addiction) would somehow bloom flowers of love and acceptance for him.

MEMO FROM NORMAL LAND®

"Authentic love has limits."

The Volume Turns Up

The next layer of abuse happened when the *mini*-scolding and lectures progressed into *private*, behind closed doors *verbal assaults*.

It was a confusing time because in public, Erik remained a diplomat, even charming and somewhat loving towards me. But *behind* closed doors, things were obviously changing.

Erik started doing what I called his "Angry Father Punishments." The Angry Father Punishments were behind closed doors *verbal assaults* where for *hours* Erik would raise his voice and reprimand me like an angry father towards his misbehaving child.

The Angry Father Episodes *never* happened in public. But once we were in the privacy of our home, the door would shut, and the campaign of shame and "punishment" would begin. Then for hours it seemed, Erik would scream, yell and accuse me of "horrific" things I *never* did; and worse, he wouldn't stop until I apologized for a my "bad" behaviors, real or not.

I understand that apologizing for uncommitted crimes to Erik may sound weak. Erik however, was a craftsman at *shifting the blame,* and inevitably, between his exhausting and fast-talking scolding, combined with my inability to handle conflict, Erik was able to change my truth. Before I knew it, he released himself of any accountability, and I was apologizing for actions I never did.

"Actions" like *flirting*, which suddenly became the new daily topic of interrogation, as well as the next layer of abuse.

The green monster of jealousy surfaced overnight in our relationship and with it, Erik's obsession with where I was, how I dressed, or worse if talked to other men.

I had never been the flirtatious type, nor had I ever given Erik a reason to be jealous, but that didn't seem to matter. Erik's new technique of interrogating and then convicting me of crimes I never committed was suddenly our new base for normal.

In her book *Co-Dependent No More*, author Melody Beattie shares that if you put a frog in boiling water, the frog will jump out to save its life. But if you put a frog in room temperature water and slowly bring up the heat, the frog will boil to death. The reason the slow heat kills the frog is because the frog loses its ability to sense the one degree shift of danger.

I share that analogy because the progression of abuse is just like the frog, the water, and the heat. Combine all three elements quickly and we abuse victims would probably run like a cat on a hot tin roof. Bring up the heat slowly, however, and before you know it, we too have lost our ability to sense danger; and with it, the impending doom that's threatening our life.

Public Humiliations

Journal Entry - November 14 (year 2 in the abuse)

"...Tonight I experienced the most humiliating and frightening moment imaginable. I am convinced the man hates me. No one can treat another person like this unless motivated by hate. I want to get away from him, but I am afraid what he might do if I try..."

It was a September evening at a going-away party when the abuse took on its next layer. That was the night the *private* verbal assaults went *public*.

I met Erik at a house party after work, and when I arrived he was, unfortunately, drunk. Not a little relaxed, or a little tipsy. Erik was edgy, angry and most apparently, drunk.

He didn't say "hello" when I entered the room. Instead, with his Jack Daniels in hand, he glared at me from across the living room. I in turn instinctively did a mental inventory and had a brief moment of relief, because I *knew* I was dressed according to "the requirements."

Erik, however, was *still* visibly upset, and without breaking his glare, he pivoted his body at me and headed my way.

I'll never forget those few long seconds as he was coming at me: Friends were talking. The room was buzzing with music. But the only sound I heard was my pounding heart and anxious breath pulsing inside my ears. Erik was in a state I had never seen him before. His eyes were back-lit with *hate;* and for reasons I did *not* understand, *that hate was coming directly at me.*

"YOU HAVE NO CLASS! YOU HAVE NO CLASS!" Erik suddenly screamed as he shoved his finger in my face and towered his body over mine.

I honest to God didn't understand what was happening. I had arrived only a few minutes earlier, and suddenly I was the center of negative attention; the focal point of almost 50 people, abruptly silenced because of Erik's rage.

In hindsight, I know I should have responded to Erik

differently than I did that night. For example, I should have shoved my finger back in his face and screamed that *he* was the one with "no class." I should have publicly told him that he did *not* have the right to speak to me that way. I should have spit on his shoes and walked out of the room, *never to speak to him again.*

But I didn't.

I didn't because I was startled and embarrassed. I didn't because I was literally speechless. I also didn't because I knew if I screamed and got "big," Erik would most definitely get *bigger,* and I had no idea what *that* would look like. Quite honestly, I wasn't ready for the outside world to see Erik's dark side; both, for his sake as well as mine. So, that's why rather than defend myself or take a step of dignity and self-respect, I did what I knew best, *which was to put on a pageant smile,* excuse myself from the staring crowd, and calmly head towards my car.

When I walked outside three of Erik's Wrecking Crew friends were there and grabbed my arm and chuckled, "Come on Tracy, Erik doesn't mean it. Sometimes he just gets a little overly excited, especially when he is drunk." But trust me when I say that Erik was more than just a little *"overly excited."* Erik was enraged and acting crazy and worse; he was coming at me again.

"WHAT THE *FUCK* WAS THAT ALL ABOUT!" He screamed as he headed towards me. "WHAT. THE. *FUCK*! DON'T YOU *EVER* WALK AWAY FROM ME LIKE THAT AGAIN!"

My head was spinning from the insanity: I was trying to get in my car and leave; his friends were holding my arms and laughing; Erik, for the first time was screaming at me in public; people were staring, and I was becoming more and more humiliated by the second.

All I wanted to do was leave. All I wanted to do was *get this very private moment out of the public eye.* But Erik would not hear of it. He blocked my car door and refused to let me depart.

I begged Erik to move away from the car, but his response was, "No way in Fucking Hell." I then begged him to get in my car and leave the party with me. But in classic Erik style, he puffed his chest and refused, claiming "Men who let women drive are *sissies.*"

I then turned to his friends and pleaded with *them* to drive Erik home, however, he wouldn't hear of that either. He threatened to "kick their asses" if they tried to take his keys, *which* was probably true; and frankly, they weren't up for a bloody street brawl *with one of their best friends.*

The situation had gotten completely out of control, so in a last-ditch effort to *regain* control I did what many tool-less women do: I awakened my inner Succubus. Meaning, in a blink of an eye, I went from a crying, scared, powerless victim, to a confident, alluring and *in control seductress.* A seductress who after a few minutes of flirtatious smiles and soothing sexual promises, single-handedly convinced Erik to leave the party with me. Which surprisingly, he agreed to; and which in an odd way felt amazing to have that control.

I got in my car and trust me when I say, *I wanted to drive off and disappear.* But Erik, in almost a mind reading way, pointed his long finger in my face and told me to, "not fuck with him." He threatened that if I *didn't* follow him home, he would "come after me." And unfortunately, I *knew* he was serious as Erik had *already* come after me once before.

The incident happened one night after I tried to leave his house during an escalated verbal attack. I got in my car after the incident and appropriately left. But he, like a madman out of Hell, came after me and car chased me into a dead-end street. He cornered me for over an hour and would not let leave until I agreed to accept his apology. Which to make the drama stop, I finally did.

So that evening, as much as I wanted to drive away, I fearfully didn't. I instead followed Erik to his house, and that was when my new degree of Hell began.

To say that Erik yelled at me that night does not quite describe it. It was more like he verbally "went nuts" on me, pacing and screaming at the top of his lungs until his face turned red, and his veins bulged from beneath his fair skin.

That night, he repeatedly threw his finger in my face, and antagonistically *jabbed* it into my shoulder. Pushing me across the room with bully-like shoves until he backed me into a corner, a corner where he would then slam his fists into the drywall next to my head leaving baseball-sized holes as the evidence of his rage.

To this day, I can't tell you *why* Erik was so enraged. All I really remember was that my fear and shock was so intense that to survive the moment, I went deep inside myself. So deep that I turned his raging screams into a mere buzzing sound in my ear; an actual distant background noise, drowned out by my own pleading thoughts that repeated, "Please God, let him fall asleep. Please God, just let him fall asleep."

I didn't realize it at the time, but that night in the depths of my terror, I learned my first form of emotional protection from abuse: *I learned how to shut down, and go within, until the attack was over.*

Erik's verbal assault lasted two hours, maybe more. Then finally between the over consumption of alcohol, and the physical drama of the episode, he collapsed in complete exhaustion.

You would think, at the first site of him sleeping I would have immediately left. But I didn't. I was still in emotional shock, and more so, I was too scared to move. I feared if I woke the bear, the cycle might start again, and I *didn't* want to go another round. So rather than leave or run for my life, I instead sat like a quiet church mouse, holding onto the sides of my chair, not even allowing the sound of my breath to make noise.

For nearly two hours I sat in that chair watching the red letters of the digital clock. Then finally, when fully convinced Erik was out for the night, I carefully, as though walking on eggshells, slipped out of the room, vowing that I would *never* return to this insanity again.

5

The Sweet Talking Words
(& Other Warning Signs)

MEMO FROM NORMAL LAND®

"Warning signs are not just signposts on the road of life.
They are roadmaps for the protection of your life."

I would like to tell you I walked out of Erik's life that next morning, and never returned. But obviously, as there is more to the story, I didn't.

In my pathetic defense, I didn't change my mind and took Erik back on account of his over-used apologies or excuses of drinking too much. (I prepared myself for those dramatics). It also wasn't his stalking levels of positive attention (something called Love Bombing) that made me consider a second chance.

The emotional kryptonite that softened my heart, and ultimately made me put down my guard, was that for the first time since knowing Erik, he showed a side of himself I didn't know existed. Meaning, from the day after the incident, the once controlling, "rage-*ohlic*" bully, suddenly turned into a meek, child-like, broken-spirited man. A broken man who (on his knees, no less) would beg, whimper and cry by saying, "Oh, Baby, no. Please don't leave me. Please don't leave."

I must admit, this *new* Erik disarmed me. I thought after the incident he would be relieved to get me out of his life.

But much to my surprise, Erik didn't feel relief at my departure, whatsoever. In fact, Erik was distraught, disjointed and most evident, *determined* to do "whatever it took" to win me back. And win me back, he tried.

Starting the day after the incident, Erik began filling my house with flowers; overloaded my voicemail with tearful phone calls of apology, and wrote me letters oozing in promises of change. Week-after-week he pleaded for my forgiveness, all while confessing his "sins" to both his friends, me and anyone who would lend him an ear.

For over a month Erik made his campaign of apology by saying things like, "I understood him, like no one else did", or "Life was *not* the same without me." Then much to my destruction, he delivered the fatal words that gave me the power to get on that crazy horse again: Erik said, he *needed* me for his life to feel *complete*.

Never before had I seen or heard anything like this. Here was a man, who had not shed a tear in his adult life; who barely showed emotion over his tragic childhood. Yet, *now* this man could not stop crying over the thought of *me* not being in his life?! It was quite the ego boost for a broken soul like me.

During that Season of Apology (professionally known as The Honeymoon Period) Erik promised that he would never yell at me again. He promised he would never humiliate me, again. And he promised he would never drink again.

In hindsight, I should have said, "Promises, promises." But instead, high on the emotion of denial, I looked the chameleon in the face, and said the forsaken word, "Forgiven."

Journal Entry - October 15 (year 2 in abuse)

"... Things have been going well for a while. Perhaps he has changed. In fact, tonight he called and told me he didn't deserve a woman like me! I think he is really starting to appreciate me..."

One of the many promises Erik made after we reconciled was to get a more responsible job; which he did by taking a management position with a new company, *three hours away.*

His transfer put us in a long-distance relationship where, for a year and a half, *I* commuted six hours a week to see him, for only *one* day a week!

On the surface, throughout our one-and-a-half-year trial stage, Erik appeared to keep his promises of change. So on the evening of my 24th birthday; on the first of what would be many Las Vegas trips, Erik surprised me with a ring, and a proposal. And I, thinking everything *had* changed, said "Yes."

Journal Entry - April 5 (year 2 in the abuse)

"I wish life could give me a sign if I am doing the right thing. Something... anything... just a sign, that will let me KNOW I am doing, the right thing... "

Erik was anxious to get married, and in four months from our engagement, I found myself walking down the aisle. I, however, was not celebrating.

You could say a lot happened during those four passing months. For starters, my mother left the country for an extended business trip. My father was a mess after the divorce. Erik was in a car accident where his spinal cord was punctured, and he was unable to walk for a week. And I, on top of my six-hour weekly commute, was working *three* jobs to pay for the Hawaiian Honeymoon, and Irish Catholic wedding; that *he and his mother were planning.*

I say "he and his mother" because the two, not Erik and I were planning our wedding. Not, however, by my choice.

You see, my vision for my ideal wedding was to get married *where* I wanted, by *whom* I wanted. My vision was to have only loved ones' present during the exchanging of the most intimate vows of my life; vows (may I add) that I could write myself. My vision was to have the ceremony be an emotional celebration of love, as well as, a *spiritual* celebration of faith and family. But as for this wedding, my wishes were not a consideration at all.

From the start, Margaret objected to almost everything I wanted, beginning with the location of the wedding. Margaret was upset that I wasn't Catholic, and she refused to attend the wedding unless it took place in a Catholic Church. She claimed that in the "Eyes of the Lord" we would not be married, if it wasn't in *The Church.*

I tried to explain my side to Margaret. I tried to share that I wanted to be married on the beach, not in a church with walls. I tried to explain that my desire was to have the ceremony officiated by someone who personally knew me, instead of by a priest who was a stranger. And most important, I tried to explain that God would "recognize" our marriage *anywhere*, as He was *not* deaf, dumb or blind. He was "God", after-all.

But none of that mattered. Margaret insisted she would not attend the wedding if it were not in the Catholic Church. So in the effort to keep the peace, a Catholic Church wedding it would be.

The next battle on Margaret's list was my bridesmaid dresses. My dream was to have a bright and colorful summer wedding with my "pageant-girl" bridesmaids dressed in a pink, toga style, abovethe-knee cocktail dress, glamorously accented with a floor-length train (note that it was the late 80's after all). But Margaret and Erik would not hear of it. "Showing legs" in Church was a "sin", as far as Margaret was concerned. And, Erik refused to be in a wedding where "pink was present." He said pink was only for "sissies"; and therefore, he "would not allow it."

For days we went around and around, on the color selection for my wedding, and finally, after considering every option in the PMS color book, Erik refused every color except one: Irish Kelly Green.

Irish Kelly Green?! Are you kidding me?? I refused! But Erik, with his learned tactic of wearing me out until I said "yes," and my inability to say "no" and mean it; he won. Irish Kelly Green, it was.

To sidebar, I will never forget the sight when I walked down the aisle on June 3rd, and saw 16 Irish Kelly green, floor length, satin, toga-styled dresses. The girls looked more like a batch of fluorescent green pickles, than beautiful blushing bridesmaids. It was horrific!

In total, we had over 30 people in our pickled-colored wedding party. Erik insisted on having both his entire family, and the Wrecking Crew in our ceremony. This interestingly enough, was one thing Margaret did not object to.

The very last battle Margaret and I had was about the style of my wedding dress. I chose a mermaid-style, strapless gown with long white gloves and a simple, yet elegant three-foot train. But that never happened. Margaret threw a fit, claiming it was "unacceptable and sinful" to show bare shoulders in church. I was too tired and too busy to battle, so without skipping a beat, I added long sleeves and a high neck to my summer gown and sweated my way through the entire evening.

I need to add that, initially I wasn't such a push-over with Margaret. It took a while for me to cave under her, *Mother-in-Law* pressure. In my defense though, I kowtowed because, whenever I courageously bucked the system and went against her wishes, Erik would emotionally punish me *by withdrawing his love and affection.*

When I look back, it's obvious to see that Erik had begun to slip into his old ways. In hindsight, though, who was I to throw stones at his relapse? *Planning a wedding was stressful on him, you know!*

Her Name was Janet

I know pre-wedding family stress is something many brides face. And certainly, as long as the couple remains in sync, it shouldn't possess the power to ruin their wedding day, joy. In truth, Margaret's control had nothing to do with what ruined mine.

I was so unhappy because I had just discovered "Janet."

In hindsight, I really should have seen it coming; as the warning signs were there for months: Erik's increase in jealousy; his nervousness about me coming to his work; and probably most noticeable, his new, weekly conversation about "cheating."

Every week, during our first dinner together, Erik would inevitably launch a discussion about cheaters. And every week the exhausting conversation would end the same way. He would interrogate me about cheating, insinuate that women who cheat are "sluts" and "deserve to be dumped"; and I like old times would find myself defending my "non-slutty, non-cheating" innocence, to the point of tears.

It took a while for the truth about Janet to surface. But good or bad, it eventually did: Five days before my wedding to be exact.

Janet was one of Erik's cocktail waitresses, and he was having an affair with her. Did I say affair? No. It was more like he was having a full-blown relationship.

I knew nothing about Janet, and in her defense, she knew nothing about me. That was until the day Erik put in a vacation request for his wedding and honeymoon; where in return, she went to his superiors and accused Erik of rape.

Erik had to tell me about Janet (and about the rape allegations) because his job was in jeopardy. Plus, Janet had personally called me.

Erik tried to deny their relationship at first, but then 48 hours before my wedding, he handed me a two-page confession letter. In the note, he detailed how their relationship started, what she meant to him, and of course, how it ended.

In the letter (which he sent to my room at our mandated Catholic pre-wedding encounter weekend) Erik made it clear that after I read his letter, we would never talk about Janet again. He told me I was "lucky" he confessed, as most men would just "let it go." He told me I was "fortunate" to have someone as *"desirable as he was."* And he told me that I, in fact, should be "flattered" not offended, that other women "wanted" him.

Erik told me in his two-page confessional that if I were truly a Godly woman I would "forgive him with Grace." He insisted that if I authentically loved him through the eyes of God, I would accept him for his flaws, and all. Then, after two days of campaigning, like so many times before; it was somewhere between his slick words of manipulation, and the dysfunction of my beaten-down mind; I forced myself to believe Erik's crazy excuses. And, against my better judgment rather than say "we're over," I put down my sword of dignity and once again said "Forgiven."

6

The Wedding
(Saying "Yes" when all the signs say "No")

MEMO FROM NORMAL LAND®

"God only gives us what we can handle.
Everything else, is our choice."

Journal Entry - June 3 (year 2.5 in the abuse)

"...On the day that I should be celebrating, I am instead completely numb. On the day that I should be glowing, I am instead pale with shock. If only they knew the shame behind my smile."

Two days after Erik's confession letter I found myself standing at the altar. To best describe how I felt, I would say, empty. I didn't feel scared. I didn't feel sad. I didn't feel happy. I just felt empty.

I made the mistake of telling no one about Janet because I was too ashamed. I was ashamed, because I feared what others they might think of Erik for doing it. I was even more ashamed of what they might think of me for tolerating it.

If the Universe sends signs to guide us along our journey, a few hours before my wedding, I got mine. It was somewhere between getting my hair and nails done when I lost Erik's wedding ring. It was an interesting moment, because I toggled between wondering if this was my signal from the Universe; to then preparing for Erik's wrath, which had slowly started to surface again.

I eventually found Erik's ring under my car seat on the way to the chapel, which when I arrived his entire family was in an upheaval.

"Where is Erik!?" they screamed, when they saw me. Apparently, he had pulled into the parking lot, and then turned around and left.

I wanted to respond by saying, "I don't know, and I don't care." Instead, I just flashed my professional smile and headed to the Orchestra Pit to sit alone. I remember sitting on the stairs in that musty room wishing I could have a good cry. Frankly, though, I couldn't. The most I could muster was a whisper, and a lost prayer that said, "Oh God, give me the strength to forgive Erik for what he did."

In the background, the wedding coordinator interrupted my thoughts by announcing, "It is time to start!", and to tell you the truth, those words felt like the first steps of a guillotine walk. I wanted to abandon the Alter, and make a B-line out of the church. I wanted to shout over the balcony at the 250 guests sitting in the audience that Erik had been having a relationship with a cocktail waitress, and he only told me about it two days ago. I wanted to scream that things were not as they appear. I was not the beautiful blushing bride. I was pissed off and hurt, and didn't want to go through with this stupid wedding. I wanted to shout that I didn't care if I threw $40,000 out the window! My happiness, damn it, was riding on the line!

But I didn't. My pride would not let me. My fear would not let me. So rather than make a mad dash for the door, I instead put on my well-rehearsed pageant smile, and walked like a wounded soldier down the stairwell.

My fluorescent pickled bridesmaids started the procession and as they did, my father, about to walk me down the aisle, joked that we could leave. He had no idea how much I wanted to take his offer. I remember looking into his blue eyes and thinking, "Yes Dad, please let's do it. Take my hand and help me run. Get me out of here and get me safe." But again, I didn't. I just smiled back at my unknowing father, and said: "It's time for us to go, Dad." And down the aisle, we went.

Erik was exceptionally fidgety at the altar. But most noticeably, Erik was once again drunk. But of course he was. He drank an entire bottle of his favorite brew on his way to the church.

If you think I was irritated about the situation, it was nothing compared to Monsignor McGinney, the Catholic clergy Margaret insisted marry us. The Monsignor (who had an incomprehensible accent) was so offended that Erik was that he rushed our ceremony. And after a few confusing rounds of kneeling, and standing, and then kneeling again, he abruptly stopped talking and just stared at us.

An awkward silence hung in the Cathedral, until Erik finally broke the tension by asking if he could kiss the bride; where the Monsignor retorted, "If you want."

Erik gave me a quick peck on the lips and then without warning, scooped me in his arms as though I was a damsel in distress (or would that be a damsel getting ready to dash) and walked out the church.

At our after-party, Erik gave a drunkard speech where he referred to me as, "The *baddest* babe he has ever met." (REALLY?! "baddest"?!!); John Sr. got smashed out of his mind, and my father told me that my marriage would never last.

I was angry with my dad that night. He was raining on my parade. Plus, deep inside I feared, he might be right.

Our false celebration lasted only a couple of hours because Erik was inebriated, and when we finally made it to the honeymoon suite, he quickly passed out for the night.

I remember looking at Erik as he lay naked, and drunk on the bed, realizing that looking at him was like looking at a stranger. The only problem was that this stranger was now my legal husband, in both, the eyes of God and man.

Journal Entry - June 4 (The Day After the Wedding)

> *"...This can't be happening. Why is this happening? How dare she do this? How dare he do this? I can't believe that they did this! The curtain has lifted, and they have removed their masks. The faces of truth have arrived. Oh God, I do not want a role in the production..."*

And So It Begins

The next morning before we left on our Hawaiian honeymoon vacation we stopped by John Sr. and Margaret's house to drop off our wedding clothes. The house was deadly silent and for some reason, deadly empty. According to my recollection, there should have been almost 14 people staying at the house. But at that moment, there appeared to be no one. The silence and the emptiness un-nerved me.

I was the first to see the post wedding war zone. I walked into the kitchen, and rather than it look like a snapshot out of Better Homes and Garden; it looked more like a violent bar brawl gone wrong. There were knocked over stools and torn drapes on the ground; there were smeared hand prints on the sliding glass door, and worse there was partially dried blood splattered on the wall, and the tile floor. The site made my stomach drop.

I ran toward Erik, hoping I could intercept him before he saw the bloody site, but I wasn't fast enough. Margaret heard us enter the house, then came running down the stairs and dramatically fell into her son's arms. She wept and moaned and held onto Erik as though she were holding onto her *very* life. Then through her tears, she told us how "Daddy" and David got into a fight; how the police pounded on the door at 2:00 a.m.; and how she didn't know what to do.

Margaret cried and clung onto her son like *no tomorrow*. Until that was, Erik became visibly upset, opened his wallet, handed her his credit card along with, all of our hard-earned honeymoon spending money; and instructed her to get a hotel room for a few days. Without skipping a beat, she gladly accepted the donation, and immediately stopped sobbing.

Oddly enough, the wedding night incident was never mentioned again; by Erik or his family. That's because what happened that night was apparently not out of the ordinary for the Sullivans. Fist fights and credit card bail-outs, were a normal way they said, "I hate you" and "I love you" all at the same time.

If you are wondering what happened at the post-wedding party, two years later my mother, who was at the Sullivan's that night, finally told me how the bloody event unfolded.

After our reception, John Sr. invited a group of people (family members, groom's men, and some other close friends) to the house for some more celebrating. In the midst of the celebration, Desiree had a damsel moment, and ran downstairs screaming that her father had molested her. John Sr. tried to get Desiree to shut-up, and physically went after her. David then went to Desiree's rescue and jumped on John Sr., where the two of them, father and son, went to blows.

Friends and family tried to separate the father and son dual. But, given their Irish tempers and intoxication levels, the two were unstoppable. Neighbors, who heard the chaos called the police. But when they arrived, Desiree systematically intercepted them at the door, and claimed there was no problem.

The strangest part of the evening, though, was Margaret's response to the craziness. During the entire fiasco, Margaret stood in the corner of the room (the same room where her husband and son were beating each other to a pulp), and rocked and sang a lullaby to a two-month-old baby.

As all Hell broke loose around her, and her family beat each other to a bloody mess, Margaret gently and calmly sang a sweet lullaby to the newborn. In the midst of the craziness she sang:

"Rock a-bye Baby

on the treetop.

When the wind the blows

The cradle will rock.

When the bough breaks

The cradle will fall,

And down will come, Baby

Cradle and aaalll"

Part III

The Abuse

7

The Craziness

MEMO FROM NORMAL LAND®

*"When you learn to accept the unthinkable,
it changes you."*

Journal Entry - July 5 (year 3 in the abuse)

"...Something in me is changing. I feel as though I am
hollow inside... as though I don't exist... as though my life
counts for nothing..."

It was a year into my marriage when I started noticing a
change in myself. My self-esteem had drastically dipped to a new
low, and I suddenly started suffering from panic attacks and
memory blanks.

I'm sure you are not surprised to hear me say this, but
again, *much had happened during that first year of marriage.* I was
living alone in a new city with no family or connection; my parents
(after an attempt to make their marriage work) filed for divorce
(again), and after a few years of breaking into the field that I had
passionately trained for, I walked away from my life-long dream of
broadcasting.

It's not that I couldn't find a job in television. I did. I was offered a position at the local ABC affiliate. But the pay was so low, I couldn't accept the job.

You see, shortly following the wedding night fiasco, the Sullivans began a ritual of running us into credit card debt; a debt that reached the tune of $15,000 in three months. In order to financially survive, I had to abandon my dream job of broadcasting, and take a "better paying" job to stay afloat.

Six months later though, I was laid-off due to budget cuts. And let me tell you, I was devastated. Not because I *loved* my job, I was devastated because I couldn't afford to be *unemployed*. That's why I took the first job I could find, which was waiting tables for the hustle of a tip. There were only two words to best describe that season: Humbling and frustrating.

The money I made wasn't nearly enough to meet our monthly obligations, so I did what many financially desperate people do during economic difficulties: I started opening lines of credit (all in my name) to support our monthly debt load. Before I knew it, the "Rob Peter to Pay Paul" cycle had me in a full financial spin.

I kept telling myself that with the next paycheck or extra side jobs, I would pay-off the new credit cards. But that windfall never happened. Erik and his family went crazy with (as they viewed it) their new found "spending power." And within the first year of our marriage, they threw us into a massive financial debt.

To be exact, over 20 credit cards totaling a sum of $50,000 were issued in my name. The plethora of plastic included Visas (*plural*) because John Sr. "needed money"; Desiree needed a Hawaiian vacation, and Erik needed to join a "get rich quick" multi-level pyramid scheme, to get us out of debt; no less. We got

Mastercards (*plural*) to fund everything from out-of-control Vegas gambling trips, to purchasing household items we did not need, and one particular card we opened just to be able to post bail when John Sr. landed in jail, *again*. There were cards from every major department store, every local grocery store, local furniture store, and there was even a credit card from the local tire store. We opened that card (or shall I say) I qualified for the automobile loan when Erik declared he needed a new car.

I want to add that I too, needed a new car at the time. But Erik, insisted on getting the new "dream machine" (as the car salesperson called it) for himself. And let me tell you, it was a dream; a white, sexy brand new, top of the line, showroom eye catcher.

From the moment we got the car, Erik informed me that I was not "allowed" to drive it. He made it clear that it was "his car"; that it was a "man's-man" car. And most important, he made it clear that "it was not the type of car a wife should be seen in"; even though, the burden to pay for it was mainly on my shoulders.

If you're wondering if I ever resisted Erik, and the Sullivan's credit card abuse, I can assure you I most definitely did. In fact, during that first year of marriage, I complained, and cried a lot.

Erik however, had no empathy, towards me nor the situation. He instead told me I needed to, "...just get used to it." That I should, "just deal with it"; because (as he justified) I was his wife, which meant I was family; and all the extreme spending of the Sullivans was just a part of "life" with his family.

But "life" with Erik, and his family was becoming impossible for me to bear. And one day after opening the American Express bill and seeing new charges of over $5,000, I snapped. As in, I think I felt a part of my brain *sizzle* that day.

For the first time, Erik was visibly upset about how stressed I had become. Unfortunately, though, it wasn't enough to stop his family from charging on the cards, or insist they start to repay.

I am sure you're wondering why I never canceled the credit cards on my own. In my defense, I did gain the courage, once. But that choice only put me in the firing line of Erik, and his family for weeks.

I canceled the cards one morning without telling them, and within moments of the cancellation, the attacks began. I was barraged with irate phone calls from both John Sr. and Holly who, daily would scream at me about, "the stress they were facing." Desiree's new favorite nickname for me was "The Selfish Bitch", which she would loudly scream in the background whenever Erik summoned me to the phone. Margaret even called me one day from David's car, crying because her home phone was disconnected. And as for Erik? He also joined the family shame campaign by telling me that I was a sinner for, "not providing for his family" as the Bible says.

The united battle was so intense and relentless that I started feeling like an unwanted stranger in my own home. Overnight, I went from the role of wife and family member, to the outcast and the enemy, and unfortunately, I was young, alone and not strong enough to take all six of them on by myself.

Finally, one night after several weeks, I broke under the barrage of pressure, and against my better judgment, I re-issued the credit cards. The response, I must say, was quite amazing. In a matter of minutes, I went from the family *reject* to the family *hero*; and with love and acceptance; the Sullivans took me back into their fold again.

After weeks of being alienated and bombarded by their

abuse and shame, they finally stopped attacking. And let me tell you, the peace felt good. It was a relief to be out of their firing line, to not shutter when the phone rang, and most of all, to be spoken to civilly (as well as, literally) again.

I say that because during the credit card stand-off, if Erik was not yelling at me, he was punishing me with torturous silent treatments. If you have never been on the receiving end of a silent treatment, they can make you feel insane. They are like Chinese War torture in that they chip away at you; one invisible moment at a time. So when Erik made me *visible* again, both verbally and physically, the welcome home made it all *almost* worth it.

Over time, credit card spending became a norm in my marriage to Erik. Every month the Sullivans would drain us of our cash. Every month, we would not have enough money for the bare essentials. Every month, I would apply for a new credit card. And every month, Erik and his family would continue to spend.

Like a good wife, though, I learned not to complain about the Sullivan *system*. I learned as Erik instructed me to "just deal with it." Meaning, I learned not to think twice about $10,000 Christmas shopping sprees. I learned to open new cards at the first glare of anger. I learned to believe that plastic was the same as prosperity. And best of all according to Erik, I learned to do it all with a Pageant Girl smile on my face.

Like many of my lessons with the Sullivans, I learned a lot about life during that time. But one thing in particular that season taught me was that when you learn to accept the unthinkable, *it changes you.*

8

The Abandonment

Journal Entry - June 3 (year 4 in the abuse)

"...Some people think being "alone" creates loneliness. But I know different. The loneliest place in the world is being alone in your marriage..."

Perhaps things wouldn't have been so bad if Erik and I were a team. But we weren't. In my marriage, I spent the majority of time alone. My work week began at 6:00 a.m., and I did not return home until 6:30 p.m. Erik's day started at 3:30 p.m., and he would not return home until 3:30 a.m. Monday through Friday, we were together only while sleeping.

On Saturdays, we would see each other for a few hours when Erik would wake after Noon. Then, just as before we were married, Sundays were our only day together.

I learned early in my marriage to do many things alone. Special events, like my birthday or our anniversary were not a priority to Erik. In fact, he refused to celebrate our anniversary, and more often than not, he "forgot" my birthday. I always found that odd, especially since I'm born on Valentine's Day.

In defense of Erik, he did remember by birthday twice. On my first birthday he bought me (drum roll please) a sandwich maker; which may I add, he made the point to tell me he bought for himself.

The second time Erik remembered my birthday, he bought me a piano. I know that sounds *fantastic*, but it wasn't. Erik purchased the piano on my credit card. He was trying to make atonement for past forgotten birthdays, so after an erratic blind-folded car ride across town, we arrived at the music store.

I resisted the purchase of the piano at first, as I had not played in over four years. Plus, it cost $3,500 which we did not have.

My resistance though, only aggravated Erik, and it wasn't long until he was yelling and screaming at me in front of the store clerk and on-looking shoppers. He yelled that his bonus check was coming, and that he would pay off the credit card immediately. He screamed that if I were a "good wife", I would let him do something nice for me. And he publicly shamed me, saying that I always ruined *everything;* over my concern for money.

To end the humiliation campaign, I gave in against my better judgment, and reluctantly signed on the dotted line. Later that month as Erik said, his bonus check *did* arrive. But to be expected, it didn't go towards the piano credit card bill. It instead went to the Sullivans. Yet, like a "good wife," I never complained about the false promise sold to me.

Double Standards

A double standard is a situation where two people are

treated differently under the same circumstance; in that, one party receives benefits, special treatment, and perks, but the other doesn't; hence, is unfairly treated.

Abusive relationships are anchored in double standards, and in our relationship birthdays, were just one of them. Erik considered my birthday "a non-event" (as he would call it), but his on the other hand was called *"The Holiday."*

Regardless of the money I had (*or not*), out of love and obligation I always planned for "The Holiday." It was important to Erik to celebrate his birthday. And it was equally important for me to make Erik happy. So every year, after doing whatever I could to do to get extra money, I always made sure there were extra funds to celebrate "The Holiday."

The first year we were married, I had a surprise Wrecking Crew dinner, and weekend party for Erik and his friends. In general, I got "good marks" for that event; minus the restaurant I chose for dinner; which Erik did not enjoy.

The next year, I had a private limousine take us, and the Wrecking Crew to Los Angeles to see Phantom of the Opera production. Unfortunately, Erik hated the entire evening; including the restaurant, the opera and the limo. Which he made sure to let me know.

The following year, when we were completely financially broke, I called a friend who owned a hotel in Ensenada, Mexico. He offered us a complimentary weekend suite, and we (Erik, me and a Wrecking Crew couple) ventured south of the border to celebrate "The Holiday." But, again, Erik was not happy about his birthday *gift*. He thought I arranged the trip for myself. If he only knew I had no idea how to spell *that* word anymore.

The last birthday we celebrated together (his 30th) I had another surprise party for Erik. The evening started with dinner with 20 of his closest Wrecking Crew friends, followed by a party at a desert resort. The evening ended with a private celebration in the master suite overlooking the pool. I'll never forget the gift his Wrecking Crew friend Pauley presented him that year: A shiny compact handgun, bullets and all. The sight of Erik holding that gun made my blood run cold.

I suppose the stress of *"The Holiday"* would have been much more manageable had it not been layered on top of THE Holidays.

Christmas, as I have brushed upon, was a mandatory celebration for Erik, and initially, I assumed the extravagant gift exchanges would be the worst of it. I, however, was wrong. After John Sr. had moved his family from California to Florida, Erik informed me that "I would not be seeing my family for the holidays *anymore*."

I immediately objected to his one-sided, double standard. But in no uncertain terms, Erik dictated that there would *never* be a Christmas where he wouldn't be at the side of *his* "Ma." He claimed she *needed* him; that her heart would break if he were not there. And he made it clear, that he would *never* do anything to hurt his "Ma."

I tried to reason and even compromise with Erik. "What about *my* mother?" I asked. He looked at me with disgust, and in his curt and condescending manner said, "What the *fuck* about your

Mom? What the *fuck* about your family? They are failures.
Remember, they are divorced."

During my marriage to Erik I didn't see my family again
during the holidays; as every year we would board a plane, and
venture to the other side of the country to be with the Sullivans.
Every year, we would exchange extravagant gifts no one could
afford. Every year Erik would leave me 10 out of the 11 days to
enjoy his vacation. And every year, John Sr. would get smashed out
of his mind, and cause a bloody family fight and ruin the entire trip.

9

The Rules

Journal Entry - September 20 (year 4 in the abuse)

"... I don't recall signing up for his rules; his ever-changing do it right or get punished" rules..."

By the second year of my marriage, my internal emotional pains started to manifest themselves physically. For example, I was nervous and anxious *all* the time. I developed strange fear-based phobias like car rides, phone calls, and even the sound of my name caused me stress. I began having sleep issues, first with insomnia where I could *not* sleep, and then with night terrors, that would not allow me *to* peacefully sleep. I suffered from chronic headaches, backaches, body aches and chronic constipation.

Behaviorally, I also started to show shifts and changes within myself. For example, I developed a slight stutter that made me feel insecure. And oddly enough, I began to tell "white lies."

They were little white lies, like whether I went to the bank at a particular time; what I ate for dinner; if I bought a lotto ticket on a certain day for him; or what time I returned home from the grocery store. *Five minutes was the difference between getting verbally and emotionally punished, and being rewarded with peace.*

I convinced myself that my lies were not really "lies" per se. Instead, they were more like moments where I *withheld* the truth to avoid punishment. I learned by the second year of my marriage that it was easier to tell a small white lie to protect myself than it was to be yelled at, for hours over something as small as purchasing the wrong *size* of Chips Ahoy cookies.

If you hadn't noticed, by year two, life with Erik was like sleeping with the enemy. His temper had reemerged, and on a daily basis, the *little things* would send him into a rage.

When I say little things, I mean little things like the toilet paper getting hung "the wrong way"; or his not getting his *immediate* wish or demand; or a big trigger was me parking the car crooked. Or shall I say, not parking it *perfectly* straight?

There were many nights when at 3:30 in the morning, Erik would yank me out of bed to show me my "sin"; demand that I apologize, and immediately go re-park the car "correctly."

The Silent Rules

In abusive relationships, there are emotional elephants that consume the relationship called *Silent Rules*. Silent Rules are the ever present, ever-narrowing, and *consistently changing* set of non-logical and unspoken rules that an abuser slowly implements to gain control over their victim. The goal of Silent Rules is to put the victim into a chronic state of stress and narcissistic focus, so there's no energy left to address the problems destroying the relationship.

Silent Rules are *never* openly voted on or agreed by both parties in the relationship. Instead, they are "learned" by the victim via trial and error; who, when gets them right has moments of peace and acceptance. Or gets them wrong and is punished.

In my relationship with Erik, when I got his Rules right, life was good for me. Erik was happy. There was peace in the home and life was "perfect"; At least according to Erik's standards.

When I got The Rules wrong, though; or when I was frustrated and *purposely* broke the rules to be my own person, *I would painfully pay the price:* Glares, scolding, silent treatments, the *threat* of him getting angry, or the reality of him *being* angry. Erik made sure I got my punishment one way or the other, whenever I broke his Rules.

I always knew when I broke one of The Erik Rules; as Erik would put me on notice by shouting my first and middle name. *"Tracy Lynn!"* he would say in a warning and summoning voice. Then, with his Angry Father Punishment, he would scold and reprimand me like a three-year-old, pointing out my obvious "stupidities" (as he named them); calling me a "bad wife"; and shaming me because of my inability to "get life right."

My List of Silent Rules

Silent Rules governed every area of my life with Erik, and though I detested everything about The Rules, there were two things in particular, I disliked the most.

The first was that if, and when I got The Rules wrong, I paid the price.

The second thing I detested was that the stupid things only applied to *me.* One time I foolishly questioned Erik on the Silent Rule Policy, and let me tell you, I paid a terrible price for asking. *That* day I learned The Rule that *challenging* Erik on the unspoken rules *broke* one of The Silent Rules. According to Erik, "*he* was the boss," and as the boss, he didn't take instructions or "lip" from anyone.

Erik had a rule for almost every area of my life. For example, some of my life-limiting rules included:

- Not making "noise" while Erik was in the house.

- *Never* disrupting Erik's sleep (though he was allowed to disturb mine).

- Not allowing my lips to touch the mouth of my water bottle as Erik did *not* want exposure to any of "my germs."

- I was not allowed to clean the house when Erik was at home. The smell of bleach and the noise of the vacuum interfered with his TV time.

- Interfering with his TV time or touching the television remote was a violation of one of The Rules as well.

- I was not allowed to eat sushi. That Rule was implemented just "because."

- I was not permitted to cut my hair or God forbid, gain weight. He threatened to kick me out of the house if the scale or the scissors tipped out of balance either way.

- I was not "allowed" to go out with my friends at night. If I did, it meant that I was a "slut."

- But for that matter, so was wearing lingerie, *even if it was with him.*

- A big rule that prompted *big* punishments was the "Keeping Silent" Rule. That rule stated that I was not allowed to voice my frustrations or opinions in *any* way about *anything* in the relationship or the family.

The Keeping Secrets rule was a catch 22 for me because if I

spoke to Erik about my concerns, he considered it "nagging." If I spoke to anyone outside my marriage, he considered it near treason. Our private life, according to Erik was "our" private life and sharing any part of it was a betrayal of loyalty to the Sullivans.

In addition to my rigid Home Rules, there were also specific *Man Rules* that Erik set for me. According to the Man Rules, I was to never:

- Make reference to another man, *even if that man was on TV or in a magazine.*

- Wear make-up if I was going to the store, as doing so meant I was trying to attract another man's attention, and that made me a "slut."

- I was not allowed to make eye contact with other men. If I did I was "flirting" and Erik was quick to remind me that only "sluts" flirt.

- I was not allowed to wear clothes that "showed the tits" (as he called them). According to Erik, they were *his*, and no man was *ever* to see them.

- The most important Man Rule Erik had, was that I was *not* permitted to have a past. In fact, shortly after we married (in one of his jealous rages) Erik destroyed all my junior high and high school yearbooks. He didn't approve of the writings and photos from my past male friends, so he ripped them to shreds.

I was sad when Erik destroyed my high school memories. But losing chunks of my childhood at that time was not worth taking another round of his jealous-bent punishments.

MEMO FROM NORMAL LAND®

"We all have a right to have a past."

Put Up Rules

There were two types of Rules that governed my relationship with Erik. There were the set of rules that strictly applied to *me; and came at the expense of me*. Then there were the rules that applied to Erik, designed for the sole *benefit* of Erik. Professionally these rules are called *Put-Ups*, and some of my Put-Up Rules included:

- Erik never going to the grocery store.

- Erik never cooking.

- Erik never cleaning the house.

- Erik wearing the nicest clothes, meaning we always had to have the budget for him to get whatever he wanted, whenever he wanted.

- Erik driving the better car; a car may I add that "had to be as sexy as he was."

- Erik never having to let me know his schedule; like when he was coming home or where he was going.

- Erik talking about things only *when* Erik wanted to talk about them, which was always, "not now."

- Erik being able to watch whatever he wanted on TV, whenever he wanted, even if I was in the middle of a show.

- And one of Erik's "favorite" rules, as he put it, was him being able to comment on other women sexually, and me not say anything about it.

The Birth Control Rule

As both a Catholic and a control freak, one of Erik's strictest rules was The Birth Control Rule. Erik was obsessed with getting me pregnant, therefore any form of birth control according to him, was not permitted.

I "disobeyed" Erik once on The Birth Control Rule and behind his back, I went on the pill. My doctor suggested I do it for my peace of mind, so I did.

My pill-popping secret lasted two weeks. Then one night when the stress of hiding and sneaking got to be too much, I decided to throw the pills in the trash.

It was 4:00 in the morning when suddenly my blankets were ripped off my sleeping body. Erik was towered over me, screaming obscenities and shoving something in my face. I was dazed and confused.

"*What the FUCK is this! WHAT-THE–FUCK is this!!*" He screamed as he threw the pills at my face.

That night I learned that Erik had an evening ritual of going through my trash after he got home. During this particular bin surveillance, he apparently found my half-empty packet of pills. And he was enraged.

My stomach dropped, and I frantically went into explanations. I tried to tell him that I was not ready for a child and that it was not fair that I didn't have any input on the situation. I tried to explain that I went on the pill because I was scared of getting pregnant, that quite truthfully our relationship was not ready for kids. I tried to explain how I came to my own conclusion that going on the pill behind his back was "wrong"; but that I went off it, because I could not stand the secrets any longer.

I tried to explain, but I couldn't. Erik was beyond enraged. He was yelling and screaming; pacing the floor and shoving his finger into my face and shoulder. Plus, he had that look in his eye that I feared: The look that told me if I moved wrong, I might be his next bloody victim.

Erik was about thirty minutes into his tyrant, then much to my surprise, he suddenly stopped yelling, looked me directly in the eye, and stormed out of the room. He went into his office, slammed the door, and then punched the wall three times. Then, much to my discomfort, the house went deadly silent.

I have to say; his silence scared me more than his rage. What was he thinking? What was he doing behind that closed door? Did he have the gun? Was he going to come after me?

My mind was racing, my heart was pounding, and my body was frozen in fear. But all that changed when the office door creaked and the sound of his approaching footsteps broke the silence in the house. *As fast as I could,* I dashed out the back bedroom door, gathered my dogs in my car and drove around the desert until the wee hours of the morning.

10

The Expected Perfection

Journal Entry February 12 (year 5 in the abuse)

"... I really don't understand this game we are playing. I am never allowed to be the best, yet I am always expected to be perfect. How is that even humanly possible?"

In 1991 the Dallas Cowboys did *not* make it to the Super Bowl. I know that sports fact, *not* because I'm a Dallas Cowboy fan, but more so because Erik was.

I remember that game so vividly because when the Cowboys failed to qualify for the Super Bowl that year, I paid the price: A one week silent treatment in our house because I watched the game with him and apparently "brought him bad luck."

A year later in 1992, Dallas made a comeback and not only made the playoffs, but they went all the way to the Super Bowl. The bad news is that they *lost* that game in the final moments.

I can still recall exactly where I was when they lost. I was standing in the TV section of the local department store. That season I learned the survival skill of "disappearing" during football season. Meaning I would leave to the shopping center, my office, *anywhere but home* whenever the Cowboys played.

That afternoon as I stood in the room full of blaring

televisions and the buzz from the final clock sounded, I started to cry and talk at the television screens. "Why?! *Why* did you have to lose?!" I said outloud. A friendly male shopper next to me said, "Hey lady, it's only a game." But with tears in my eyes, I looked at him in despair and said, "I wish that were the case."

I learned early in our marriage that Erik took losing *very* personal. But of course, he did. He was a narcissist and a perfectionist, and like both, he viewed the success or *failure* of anything associated with him as a direct reflection of himself. It didn't matter if it was a board game, video games, sports, or even a silly round of Marco Polo in the pool. The Silent Rule that governed our world stated that "Erik must *always* win"; and *anyone* who broke that rule paid a terrible price for his ego bent loss.

I, unfortunately, learned *that* lesson the hard way when one time during an innocent game of one-on-one basketball, I beat Erik. No, that's not the total truth. I smeared him, 10 – 1. But let me tell you, I paid a hefty price for it: Yelling, shaming, and name-calling. He made sure I got my punishment for coming in first.

Participating in group sports or one-on-one *anything* with Erik was always a bitter-sweet dynamic. On one hand, I *loved* watching Erik when he would win and have his moment of victory. He would gloat, laugh and parade around like the child he was never able to be in his youth. When he would lose, though, or when someone was just better at something than he was, the loss would launch him into a child-like temper tantrum where without mercy he would bash and publicly punish his victor for their success.

I asked Erik once why he took loss so personal. He said it was because he was a "Sullivan"; an "Irishman" as he called himself. And any loss, no matter how small, he viewed as a slam against his character.

The Animals

As a Perfectionist, Erik had an impossible bar of expectation for both everyone and *everything* around him; which included me, his employees, and believe it or not, even our dogs.

Though Erik claimed he wanted animals, it never made sense to me, as according to him the animals made "him nuts." Their fur made him "nuts." Their barking made him "nuts." Their dog behaviors, like pooping, digging or chewing, made him "nuts." But then again so did "their breathing", "their scratching" and "their dirty dog bowls."

Our dogs, unfortunately, paid the price *a lot* with Erik. If he was in a "mood" and they irritated him, he would violently airlift them by the collar, drag them with their hind toenails scratching the floor, then *thew* them in the backyard.

I always ran after the dogs to make sure they weren't injured. That however only infuriated Erik and one time after I went to care for them; he slammed the door and locked me out of the house for hours as well.

Over time our dogs grew afraid of Erik. In fact, so frightened that they would run and hide whenever they heard his car pull into the garage. I can't begin to tell you the number of times I wanted to run and hide with them as well.

Erik and I had three dogs together and all three irritated Erik to an extent. But he was most bothered by my white female Samoyed, named Skitaka.

Erik considered Skitaka "my dog" and I guess she was, as many nights when I was crying over something Erik did, Skitaka would curl next to me and catch my tears on her furry white back.

Our dogs sadly took a lot of unnecessary abuse over the years, and for the longest time I couldn't figure out if Erik's aggression was on account of their dog-like imperfections? Or were the assaults on them, on account of me? I couldn't help but wonder, if when he kicked at them, was he kicking at *"them*?" Or was it a sign of how he would treat our unborn children if their innocent human flaws bothered him? I guess in hindsight; happiness, is never knowing.

The Pedestal of Perfection

When you live with a Perfectionist, there is a complicated dynamic that plays havoc with your sanity and self-esteem. It's a dynamic I call the *Perfectionist's Pedestal Syndrome*. It's where a Perfectionist puts you on a pedestal, and you're *expected* to be perfect. But it's a pedestal where you are never allowed to *be* the best.

Erik had me on his Perfectionist's Pedestal. And it didn't matter if it was cooking, shopping, or a simple game of golf with his friends; if I didn't do things according to Erik's standard of "right", my *"wrong"* got labeled as "lame", "uncoordinated" or one of his favorite statements, "an embarrassment as a wife."

I remember the first time I made Erik's favorite "Beef and Noodles" dinner. It was a meal his "Ma" used to make that took over 3 hours to prepare. He tasted it, threw his fork on the plate and barked with disgust, "This is not like my Ma's." He then pushed his plate away, threw his napkin on the table, and that is when the shame campaign began. He called me a "bad wife" for cooking it wrong. He told me that "my mother must have taught me nothing on how to care for a man." And then proceeded to lecture me for a half-an-hour about the type the qualities a "real woman" has.

You might wonder if I stood there and took Erik's verbal beatings at moments like that. I didn't; that is, *on the inside.*

Many times when Erik made his ridiculous comments and judgments, my inside voice would snap back at him and say. *"No, King Erik! I never learned how to spend three hours making Beef and Noodles; because unlike you, I was a little busy getting a college degree in my twenties!"*

That particular night, though, I didn't dare vocalize those words. I was smart enough, or better stated, *conditioned* enough to know it would only make the episode bigger. I was tired after a long day of work and I had to be up at 6:00 a.m. So instead of defending my truth, speaking my mind, holding my ground or whatever you want to call it, I opted to remove the Beef and Noodles from the table, opened the refrigerator and found something else to make for his 10:00 pm dinner.

My Body

Erik expected me to be perfect in all areas of my life, but his strictest expectation was with my body. Erik constantly told me I was fat, even after I won Mrs. California at a size 3. According to him, my breasts were never large enough, my stomach was never flat enough, and my arms were never muscular enough.

By year three of our marriage, Erik had become generous about discussing my "inadequacies", (as he would call them) in private. But one weekend while at a wedding party, he decided to "go public."

I was lying by the hotel pool when Erik summoned me to join him and his friends at the bar. Like a trained, scared puppy I immediately obeyed. I remember standing in front of Erik waiting to hear what he needed. Then, at a mere 109 pounds (I'm 5' 7") he began his *public humiliation*: He informed all who could hear that "in *his* opinion" he considered me "pretty", but without a doubt, terms my "tits" were not big enough for a "real man." The Public Humiliation was nothing short of devastating embarrassment.

Erik had a ritual of chipping away at my natural C-cup "inadequacies", as he called them, and he consistently compared me (or *failed* me) to "real women." So it was somewhere between the constant criticism and the *non-refundable gift of "new boobs"* (as he stated) that I finally and reluctantly agreed to the breast augmentation surgery.

I didn't tell anyone about the surgery, except my mother; *who I informed only the morning of the operation.* She was furious. She knew I was doing it for Erik, not for myself; which, she was one hundred percent correct.

The surgery was much more painful than I had expected and to make matters worse I had an adverse reaction to the anesthesia. This, unfortunately, delayed my recovery by 45 minutes, where in turn, Erik had no choice but to wait.

Needless to say, Erik was *furious* when I came out of the recovery room and rather than ask if I was *okay*, he instead glared at me, then snapped at the nurses to "hurry up."

He was in some mood that day. But nothing prepared me for what happened next. After the silent car ride home (where of course I had to apologize for getting sick and causing the delay) Erik put me in bed, handed me a bottle of pain pills along with a glass of water, and then informed me he was *leaving*.

"Leaving?!" I gasped in my foggy state. "Erik, you can't leave. I need you! I can't get out of bed on my own. I need you to help take care of me! Erik..." I pleaded, "Please, don't leave me now."

Erik said something about having a headache and needing to go to the hospital. He then gave me one more set of instructions, tossed the second jar of pills on the bed and walked out of the room.

I have to admit I didn't believe Erik was serious about *leaving* me. Three hours later, though, when I woke to what felt like *knives* thrusting into my chest, I realized he was.

Skitaka, my sweet Samoyed had jumped on the bed and landed on my bandages. I screamed in agony. She and my other two dogs *yelped* in desperation. They had been locked in the house for hours and urgently needed to go outside.

Before I continue, allow me to sidebar for a moment. If you have never had a breast augmentation surgery, there is one thing you need to know about the procedure. After surgery you do not have *any* upper body strength; that, and *every* muscle from your stomach to your brain hurts.

I didn't know that little caveat about the surgery and in my ignorant and groggy state I attempted to push myself into a sitting position on the bed; only to gasp and literary collapse backward in piercing pain. I then tried to roll over on my side, which thank God I did, but once there I didn't have the strength to sit myself up.

For 10 minutes I fought with myself, sweating, tearing, and feeling victimized by my lack of mobility and strength. Then finally with lots of willpower (not to mention three barking dogs) I maneuver myself to the side of the bed where I gallantly swung my legs *over* the mattress, *only* to have the weight of my lower body carry the rest of me to the *floor* with a hard *thud.*

The dogs were barking as if to say, "Don't stop now Mom! You are almost there! The Pee Zone is near! *Push* Mom! *Push!*" So I pushed my back against the side of the bed, used my legs to lift myself to a standing position and then exhaustedly walked to the sliding glass doors.

As the dogs ran to their grass toilet of relief I looked at the clock and realized it had been over three hours since Erik had left the house. Three more hours would pass, however, before he would contact me.

When he finally did, Erik informed me that he was still at the hospital. In fact, Erik told me that he had checked himself *into* the hospital and according to him he didn't know when he would be home.

At first, I thought he was joking. Erik knew how helpless I was from the surgery, right? *The doctor told him I needed help.* I could barely open a medicine bottle on my own, let alone take complete care of myself. *Under doctor's orders,* I couldn't drive for the next ten days, and there was barely enough food to eat in the house. Plus, he knew that I didn't have anyone close-by to take care of me, and my family was hours away. He wouldn't dare think of leaving me at a time like this, would he?

The answer was "of course, he would." Erik bluntly told me that under no uncertain terms, he was *not* coming home; that I was on my own; and that I needed to figure out how to help myself. Then without apology or explanation, he said he needed to end the phone because "they were about to serve him dinner" in his hospital bed.

Before we closed the phone, I asked Erik if he was *okay.* He told me in a matter-of-fact manner, "I have a very bad headache."

I could not believe my ears...a headache? I suffered from

migraines almost twice a month for years. I had never gone to the hospital, nor missed a work day because of them. So I begged Erik to reconsider.

But Erik, being Erik, refused. He said he needed to be taken care of, and "obviously" I was "in no condition to do it." I pleaded with him to change his mind. I tried to reason with him that I needed help. But he wouldn't budge. Erik made his decision. He "needed to be taken care of," so he was staying in the hospital. Then, in classic Erik style, he announced that the conversation "was over"; that he was "done talking about things", and then he closed the phone with a sharp click.

Erik left me alone for three days to care for myself. During that time, I learned creative ways to get in and out of bed with no upper body strength, and more insightful, I learned another Silent Rule in classic trial and error style: I learned that I was never to put Erik in the position to take care of me.

Unfortunately, changing my body didn't stop Erik's constant criticism of me. And by year three it seemed that no matter how much I exercised, or how tan I was (which was a rule he had for me) or how much I changed my physical being for the better, Erik was still dissatisfied. No matter how hard I tried to become "enough", Erik still found fault and criticism with almost every part of me: My body, my hair, my scent, my skin. He seemed to dislike almost every part of me; except that is, sex.

Erik was *obsessed* with having sex with me. Not making

love, not sharing each other's body or experiencing a moment of intimacy, passion or eroticism. Erik didn't believe in kissing. He thought it was "gross" (as he would say.) So all Erik wanted from me was *sex*: Uncaring, mandatory, missionary style sex.

If you're wondering if the rules that governed the house carried over into our bedroom, the answer is "Yes." Even our sex life had its set of controlling rules, four to be exact.

Sex Rule Number One stated that Erik was to enjoy sex, and I was to perform. Erik did not believe in foreplay or reciprocity. He only subscribed to one position, missionary style, shut-eye sex. And *anything* outside of that guideline was off-limits and forbidden.

Sex Rule Number Two stated that we were never to talk about Sex Rule Number One, because discussions about sex were off limits. According to Erik, I should be "happy" with what I got (as he would say) and asking for more or anything different meant that I was a "slut."

Sex Rule Number Three stated that I was not allowed to say "No" to Erik's sexual requests or timing. If I did, he would either call me "frigid"; or he would begin a jealous campaign, claiming that if I didn't want sex with him, I was obviously "getting it elsewhere."

Sex Rule Number Four, which was probably the most important but *impossible* one, was that I had to pretend *always* to enjoy sex with Erik. Regardless that Erik did not touch me to the point of pleasure; the rule stated that if I didn't act as though I liked it, I paid the price. All I can say to that rule is, *thank God for Meg Ryan in "Sleepless in Seattle."*

Sex with Erik was quick, mandatory and predictable. Then, unfortunately, one night, all of that changed.

I was in Las Vegas for a two-day work convention. Erik

came with me because he had an "itch" to play Craps.

Like all of our trips to Vegas, Erik disappeared late into the night. He finally returned at four in the morning and he was in a mood. Apparently, he lost a lot of money at the Crap tables and according to him (though I was not there) it was somehow my fault.

I didn't think twice about getting blamed for Erik's loss that evening. Whenever anything went wrong in Erik's life, I ultimately was to blame. For example, when Erik's body wasn't the image he wanted, it was my fault that "he couldn't make it to the gym." When Erik started going bald at the age of 27, it was my fault as "I stressed him out too much." When his attorney got $70,000 instead of $90,000 as he wanted from his car accident settlement, it was again my fault. "I stressed him out about money."

To sidebar, I am sure you are wondering about this $70,000 financial settlement. Logically you would think this infusion of money would have put us on our feet and got us back to good; or at least *back to normal*, but no. Twenty-four hours after we got the settlement check, most of the money was spent: $20,000 to David, $25,000 to Margaret and John Sr., $5,000 to Desiree and $5,000 to Holly.

Erik did, of course, keep *some* of the money in our account. In fact, he took $12,000 and used it towards a down payment on a small house for us.

Again, you would think I would be happy about that. But unfortunately, I wasn't. Erik bought the house without my seeing it, and not to sound ungrateful or crass; *this house was a crap hole.*

In fact, I nicked-named the house "The Shit Hole" not only because this house was a bit run down and outdated (and we did not have the money to make improvements). But more so because this house was in a *horrific* and unsafe neighborhood that no one *by choice* would put their wife in; especially since I spent so much time alone.

How bad was this neighborhood, you ask? Drug dealers book-ended our street; our road had no sidewalks or street lights; and may I add that our house backed-up to a barbed wire fence that "protected" us from the terrain of the California desert. Meaning, our backyard was in the wind channel of miles and miles of *blowing* desert sand; sand that blew hard enough to put pox marks our car and house windows, and sand that every day would blow a two-inch sand carpet into our backyard *pool*.

Yes, I said pool. To make matters worse, The Shit Hole, for reasons I will never understand, had a pool.

I know it sounds wonderful and very California-ish. But we could never use the pool because when the wind would blow (which was *every* day) the sand from the desert floor would spill into the pool and turn the aqua blue water into a sandy, murky, dirty mess.

While the house was still in escrow I shared with Erik that I didn't want to live in *this* neighborhood. I told him I didn't feel safe, especially since I was home alone, so often. I told him the house required too much work and that it would not appreciate in value. And need I mention my concern about the sand pool in the backyard? The one I would be responsible for cleaning?

He, though, didn't care. His response to my concern was it was "his" money, not mine. He said he was "the man of the house *with the only input that counted*." And to make matters worse, Erik told me if I didn't like the house, I could "find a new place to live."

Needless to say, I learned over the years that objecting to Erik was an effort in vain. So (fast-forward to the hotel room in

Vegas) that night when he returned and *again* blamed me for his losses at the Crap Table, I didn't object. Apparently, I brought him "bad luck" *from my hotel room*; and that, he explained is *why* he lost our house payment.

I didn't say anything to Erik about losing our house payment. I could tell by the look in his eye that he was ready to explode. Plus, he was pacing the small hotel room and loudly breathing through his nose, which meant he was ignited.

I walked into the bathroom to give Erik space, and while re-brushing my teeth, I looked up from the sink and caught Erik's reflection in the bathroom mirror. He was standing behind me in the doorway glaring. Then, with no emotion, he demanded Sex Rule Number One, by commanding "I'm horny."

My stomach dropped to the floor. I wanted to tell him *"No!"* I wanted to tell him I hated having sex with him when I was nothing more than just a release or receptacle. I wanted to tell him that I felt used when he would do this to me. I wanted to tell him that the last thing I wanted was to be close to him, especially after he recklessly lost *our* money *that we needed for our house payment.*

But by the look in his eye, I knew that tonight was not the night to challenge him. So rather than stand my ground and do what was right for me, I instead took off my clothes, got into bed, and routinely held my breath.

Erik towered over the side of the bed and informed me he wanted to try "something new." Then without warning, he proceeded to unscrew the wooden post from the headboard of the hotel bed frame. I went numb. I tried to speak, but only a whisper came out: "No Erik, you can't do that."

He continued to unscrew the bed post as though I had said

nothing. I panicked and said, "No Erik, you can't do that. It's dirty. It's germy, and you don't know whose hands have been on it."

He ignored my concern and continued to fight with the post until it dislodged. Now I was screaming, "No Erik, NO! I *won't* do that. You can hurt me with that thing. It is not a sex toy, Erik! No, please NO!"

But with the bedpost conquered, Erik looked at me and snapped. He started yelling and insulting me, telling me that I was frigid and that I needed to learn how to *"Fuck."* He towered over me and waved the bedpost in my face, almost threatening to hit me with it, where in response I started to cry.

It was as though my fear and tears were a victory to Erik, and he became aroused like I had never seen him before. I tried to move, but he violently pushed me back on the bed, pinned my body down against the sheets and carelessly shoved the bedpost inside me.

I gasped with pain. He thought I was gasping from pleasure. So he pushed it harder and harder, holding my arms and body down with his, all while breathing heavily in my ear. I thought I would throw up from fear. I thought I would faint from the pain. Instead, I used my great escape, the one I used when things got too much for me and slipped out of my reality. I closed my eyes, and I disappeared deep inside myself until Erik's sexual fantasy was over.

11

The Loss of Self Esteem

Journal Entry - March 15 (year 5 in the abuse)

"What is it about me that makes me so unlovable? Or why am I so difficult to love? It's as though the more I try, the more he hates - the nicer I am, the meaner he gets."

I'll open this chapter as I have opened previous ones by saying this: Three years into my marriage a *lot had happened.* But this time, rather than things happening *to* me, they were now starting to happen *around me.*

For example, by year three I had lost the ability to make simple decisions, even small ones like what to order at a restaurant or how much gas to put in my car. I lost my confidence at my job. And most impacting, I had also lost all of my friends.

I lost my friends because Erik, for whatever reason, disliked *all* of my friends; and one-by-one he manipulatively removed them from my circle of connection.

His push to isolate me from the outside world began like most of his abusive campaigns, which was *slowly.* This particular campaign started with a technique called *fault-finding.* Fault-finding is a control tactic where an abuser finds *on-going* fault in the things, people or activities that occupy the victim's attention. When it came to my friends, his fault-findings included objections such as, they are "divorced", "single" or of a "different religion."

His *fault-finding* then turned into personal disdain where at the very scent of them he would make disapproving comments like, "I am not comfortable being with them" or "you know how I feel about them." Which that then merged into a *direct control tactic* (and a new rule) that stated, "*I* don't want those people around this house." Or (my personal *favorite*), "I thought *we* agreed that *you* would not talk to these people anymore." Before I knew it, these "joint" rules that I never voted on or agreed to, suddenly became the new policy system for our household.

Whenever my friends or family did break the Silent Rule and visit my home, Erik was nothing short of rude. His greeting consisted of an arrogant grunt, glare or, "you're bothering me" dismissal, where *everyone* including myself, walked on eggshells around Erik.

After a while our friendships turned into only phone calls of connection. But it wasn't long until those *too* became an issue with Erik.

If and when my friends did phone, Erik would give me the "warning look" of disapproval. Or, he would raise the volume on the television so loud that I couldn't hear the conversation. Or, he would give me "The sigh", which told me that "it was time to get off the phone."

If I walked into another room to avoid disturbing Erik, he would accuse me of "having something to hide"; which inevitably lead to me somehow being a "slut." And God forbid if there was a hang-up or a wrong number on the house phone. Those launched episodes and blame campaigns that sometimes could last for hours.

Over time I eventually offended (or at minimum neglected) most of my friends and one-by-one they inevitably stopped calling. At the time it was just as well. It took a lot of energy to create the "happy front." Plus, friendships equaled punishments, and one less friendship around me, meant one less episode and punishment *for me.*

My mother luckily didn't stop visiting me during that time. But one time she shared when she left my house, she always cried. She said at the time she never understood why. In hindsight, I guess it's what you call a mother's intuition.

The Spill Over Effect

By year three it became near impossible for me to maintain the false image of perfection, and any confidence I was able to display was nothing more than a show. That was when my punctured self-esteem started to leak onto the *only* world left outside of my marriage, which was my work.

My job performance had progressively declined over the years and with it went my energy, my creativity, my initiative and my focus. My decline was a massive shift because before I was married, I *loved* to work. I had always been the company poster child, the star employee, the go-getter and "idea person" as my former bosses would say.

A few years later, though, my work character had drastically changed. For example, fear of failure replaced my initiative. Self-doubt substituted confidence; and as for respect? I began allowing my bosses to treat me in ways the former "Me" would have never permitted. If they patronized me, insulted me, took my accomplishments for themselves, or sexually harassed me, I just silently put up with it.

I often wondered during that season *why* I allowed people outside my husband to walk on me. Years later I realized it was because the effects of abuse are like an oozing scuzz. Meaning it's not something that remains isolated just between the Breaker and the Broken.

When a person lives in an environment where their self-esteem is chipped away at, they can't help but take that fractured Self into the world and establish a baseline of treatment or respect (or in truth, *disrespect*) with others. "After-all" (our fragile self-esteem reasons) "if the most important person in my life thinks so little of me, what must the average Joe-schmo think?"

It is a dynamic I call the Spill-Over Effect, and unfortunately, it's a cycle that unless stopped, puts us into an emotional slip zone. A slip zone where because we are *treated* like nothing, we start to *feel* like nothing. Then because we *feel* like nothing, we begin to *believe* we are nothing. Which that wrong belief then prompts us to *act* like nothing; which over time, prompts us to abandon our life and eventually as a result, we end-up becoming *nothing*.

12

Wanting to End it All

Journal Entry - March 15 (year 5 in the abuse)

"...As I write this, I am flying to Phoenix for a week. I used to be so scared to fly because I was afraid the plane would crash. But now as I look out the window, I think I would almost be happier if the plane did go down. At least if I were dead, the pain would stop. At least if I was dead, it would put an end to this miserable existence I call "my life..."

It was hard to believe I reached a point of wanting to end it all. Only five years earlier I was a young woman who felt I had the world at my feet.

Five years later, though, I felt like an *old* woman who the world was *dragging by the feet*. I was dazed and confused. I felt beat-up and bruised. I was so physically and emotionally exhausted I had started to believe my life was no longer worth living. And as every day passed, I found myself thinking more and more about my death.

To be brutally honest, my entertainment with death was not focused on me. It was on Erik where in the secret place of my mind, I would imagine Erik dying of some horrible disease or in some tragic accident.

Let me be clear and say that it's not that I wanted anything to happen to Erik. I just desperately wanted the pain to stop; so in my irrational mind, I reasoned that if Erik died, then all the pain would go with him. I reasoned that if *he* passed, I would not have to be the "bad person" and address the problems that felt impossible to fix.

The thoughts of Erik dying didn't continue for long because let's face it, every time I pondered about his demise I felt horrible; so un-God-like and frankly, downright demented. I mean, wives are not supposed to have death thoughts about their husbands. Wives, especially, Godly wives are supposed to be loving, submissive and never complaining (as Margaret would tell me). So rather than continue to think ugly thoughts about my husband, I made the destructive choice to turn the story line of death from Erik onto me.

And why not me? Erik had always told me that *I* was the one who caused *all* of the problems in our relationship. *I* was the one who could not "get anything right." And *I* was the only one who "constantly complained" about our situation. Didn't it make sense then, that the problem in our relationship was not Erik, but instead it was *me*?

I know most people would leave a marriage or a relationship before they reached a point of suicide. But leaving my marriage was not an option for me. I didn't believe in divorce. I thought people who got divorced lacked the guts or strength to make things work. *I thought people who got divorced were quitters,* and one thing I had never been was a quitter.

After-all, I *couldn't* be a quitter. My parents "quit"; my friends "quit". Most impacting, though, my vice grip moral code would not *allow* me to quit. "God hates divorce" was a message burned into my soul since childhood. Plus, according to my faith, wasn't I to be "long-suffering?"

The answer I thought was "yes." The answer I thought was "God can heal anything." So in my effort to do *everything* my religion required of me, I "stood in faith." I "called things not as though they were." I put oil on his pillow. I prayed over his chair. I "turned the other cheek." I tithed money I didn't have. I submitted to the point of abuse, and I even fasted and prayed until I was near anorexic.

I did *everything* the rules and regulations my faith had taught me. After three-and-a-half years, though, of *no change in sight,* it was apparent that even my faith wasn't good enough. That was when my reasoning for death made sense. Divorce was not an option. Erik would not hear of getting help. God had evidently forgotten me; and therefore, death would be the only way out of my pain.

Many nights would go by when at home alone, I held "the gun" in my hand, looked the barrel in the face and planned my exit from this Hellish place called life. I even decided where the shooting would happen. Inside my bathtub shower with the curtain closed. That way there wouldn't be *that* big of a mess. Erik hated messes, you know. They made him *go nuts.* The least I could do was keep things clean so I wouldn't upset him on my last day on earth.

Journal Entry March 21 (year 5 in the abuse)

"... Like a shooting star in a desert night, my self-worth as I once knew it, is gone. I can see remnants of it around my house: beauty pageant crowns, college diplomas, dusty recognitions of achievements from jobs long past. But now I have none of these. It has been years since I have accomplished anything. It's been years since I have done

"anything right."

I look around day-after-day wondering how I can get my self-worth back; but worse, I look around wondering how in the world I lost it in the first place..."

The physical and emotional changes in me were becoming impossible to ignore. So much, that one day I caught my reflection in the mirror, and I didn't recognize the person looking back at me.

I remember seeing myself and thinking, "Who is that person in the mirror? She looks so tired, so old, so lost, so hopeless." I remember looking at myself thinking *"Who are you?* And what happened to the vibrant young woman who only a few years earlier had dreams and visions for a grand life?"

Believe it or not, my demise didn't make sense to me. You could say it was similar to not being able to see the forest through the trees. My physical body ached, but if asked, "From *what?"* I wouldn't have been able to tell you. Emotionally I had no self-esteem, no self-value, but again, if you were to ask *"why?"* I wouldn't have been able to say.

Erik, after all, had never hit me. I never had to check myself into a hospital for broken bones. I never had to explain mystery bruises to friends and family. After five and a half years though, of Erik's life brushing up against mine, I never felt so beat-up in all my life. And I, in all honesty, had no idea *why*.

MEMO FROM NORMAL LAND®

"Ask and it shall be given."

It was Easter weekend when I made my first cry for help. Against Erik's consent, I went to see my family for the holiday.

My mother rented a beach house on the California coastline. For the first time in a long time, our family was going to celebrate the holiday together.

The weekend was a hazy blur, small talk here and a few family laughs there. It was hard for me to focus, let alone enjoy myself as I knew Erik was mad at me for leaving. I also knew there would be a price to pay for me choosing my family over him, and that lurking knowledge prohibited me from enjoying my days.

It was a spectacularly sunny day in California that afternoon, and Dana and I went to the sun deck to watch the children play on the beach below. The next thing I knew I was spilling my soul and my secrets to my older sister. For the first time, *ever* I was telling my family about my shrouded life.

I told my older sister *everything* that day. I told her about Erik's all night outings, and his frequent jaunts with hookers and strippers. I told her about my fear and panic attacks, and about the lonely nights and crazy alcoholic holidays. I told her how Erik had gambled away our household income, and how he ran me into extreme credit card debt. I told her about his violent temper and how many nights I would hide in my car to get away from his rage. I even told her that day that God had forgotten me; and how disappointed I was in realizing that.

For hours I sat next to my older sister and shared my secrets about my life with Erik, and for hours my older sister just sat next to me and listened.

When I finally purged my last backlog of pain, Dana and I

walked into the kitchen and made jelly sandwiches like we did when we were kids. Then soon after, we retired to the same bedroom where we were to sleep for the night.

I remember crawling into bed with my older sister next to me and feeling safe for the first time in years. Dana and I shared a bedroom when we were children and for almost 12 years we went to sleep together every night.

But that night, I wasn't able to fall asleep like I did as a child. My anxiety was out of control. *I had broken a Silent Rule and shared my private secrets.* If Erik found out, there would be a price to pay.

I was in the middle of my mind racing, defense-planning when Dana suddenly snuggled behind me (pregnant belly and all) and wrapped her loving arms around my frightened body.

At first, I panicked. It had been so long since someone safely held me. But like a protective big sister, she refused to let go. She caressed my hair and held me tight. Then like words from a sweet angel she whispered in my ear, "Tracy, you're God's daughter, and He doesn't want you treated this way."

I took a deep breath and closed my eyes letting the tears run down my face onto the pillow beneath my head. Then slowly as I drifted off into sleep, my older sister gently rocked me until the wee hours of the morning.

13

The Cry for Help

I would like to tell you that I headed back to the desert that next day with the courage to say "no more," but again, I didn't. I went back to Erik that weekend and just like before, right back into the insanity I knew so well. Erik ruling the house with a single glare and me behaving like a maniac, jumping out of a dead sleep at 3:00 in the morning to make sure the toilet paper got hung correctly or the car was parked straight.

As abuse is a cycle, it was only a matter of weeks until things escalated again and Erik had one of his "nuts zone" attacks.

I don't remember what sent him over the edge or exactly how many hours he raged because that night a different dynamic unfolded. Meaning, when the rage attack started, rather than disappear inside myself to survive, I instead *cracked*. Some might call it "going coo-coo." Some might call it a nervous breakdown, which maybe it was. Whatever it was, in a blink of a moment it happened to me, and I *lost* it.

Before I continue, I'm sure you're wondering *why* I didn't physically leave the house or fight back whenever Erik would rage. To answer that obvious question, I didn't leave because I couldn't leave. Erik had a habit of hiding my keys. Plus, on the few occasions I tried, Erik charged and physically held me like a prisoner trying to jump fence. As for not fighting back, I guess you could say I was well-trained. Erik knew I lived in fear *of* his temper, as well as the *unknown* of his temper. There was an unspoken, mutual understanding that he could *snap* at any moment and go into his black-out "nuts zone." The fear of *that* kept me in check.

That night, therefore, as he screamed at the top of his lungs; chest-butted me when I turned my back on him; shoved me with his finger and *pushed* me around the house like a bully on a playground, I tried to stay calm so *he* would not snap.

But before I knew it, I beat him to it. Meaning after hours of Erik *relentlessly* coming at me (with what I believe was his attempt to get physical) I finally broke; and like a Hiroshima bomb victim, I shrieked at the top of my lungs then sprinted across the house to the back bedroom. I ran behind our desk, curled myself into a human ball and then in a state of despair and terror I started to cry, rock, moan and gasp for air; and cry, rock, moan and gasp for air.

I stayed in that fetal position for two, maybe three hours, repeating to myself, "Oh my God, I think I have officially gone crazy. My God, I think I have lost my mind."

For whatever reason, Erik did not come after me anymore that night. Luckily soon after the incident, he passed out from exhaustion. I, however, did not move from my corner behind the desk. Instead, I drifted in and out of sleep until the next morning, where when I awoke, I *finally* made a decision to get myself help.

MEMO FROM NORMAL LAND®

"Problems do not go away by chance.
They go away by choice."

I didn't know what to look for in a counselor because to be honest; *I didn't know what was wrong with me.*

After a week of research, I finally found a lady named Sara who was located two hours from my house. I chose someone outside my city because I didn't want Erik to know I was seeking help, as "going to a counselor" was against The Silent Rules.

I will never forget our first conversation together. She looked at me and said, "Why are you here, Tracy?"

I told her I didn't know exactly *why*, but I did know that something was very wrong with me. I told her I was either crying non-stop, for little or no reason. Or, I was completely shut down to my emotions.

For example, I shared that my grandmother had a heart attack and almost died, and all I said was "Oh." My boss threatened to fire me. It didn't faze me. My husband, however, would glance at me from across the room, and I would tremble and break into tears.

She looked at me then wrote something on her notepad. Without glancing up she continued, "Describe how you feel on an average day?"

I paused. "On an average day? How about *every* day? It doesn't have to be a special day for me to feel what I feel. All I have to do is wake-up in the morning..."

I paused for brief second and gained the courage to speak.

"Every day now Sara, I feel blank... worn-out... numb... emotionless but way overemotional. I feel scared of love, scared of not having love... Actually I feel scared, *period*. I feel alone, lost, not in control, but totally over-controlled. I feel worried, confused, victimized, depressed... I feel like I am positively faking being positive. I feel unfocused... not in touch with myself... unable to solve my problems. I feel passive, full of excuses, shameful, and guilty...*very, very guilty*... I feel like a bomb waiting to go off... I feel secretive, worthless, hopeless and crazy. God, I hope not...I hope I'm not going crazy."

She paused for a brief moment and asked, "What are your rights in your marriage, Tracy?"

Her question stumped me.

"*My what?!*" I thought to myself. Sara, apparently reading my mind responded, "Your Rights, Tracy...your *Rights*."

I looked at her like a three-year-old being asked to solve an algebra problem. "My Rights? I... I... I don't know what you mean... I guess... I mean..." I sighed. "I don't understand what you are saying to me."

It had been so long since I had thought about *my* life and *my* needs that her question did not make sense.

She continued trying to explain. "Your *RIGHTS* Tracy. Your privileges; the things you *need* in your life to be happy, to know who you are. The things in life that let you be, you."

I thought about her question and reflected on my marriage to Erik. I did not have the *right* to practice the faith of my choice. I did not have the *right* to pursue my dreams. I did not have the *right* to express my thoughts or speak my mind. I did not have the *right* to laugh, to cry, to be happy or to be sad. I did not have the right to sleep peacefully at night. Or to eat what I wanted to eat. Or to socialize with whomever made me happy. I did not have the right to believe what I wanted to believe, to think what I wanted to think, or to be whoever I wanted to be.

I was shocked by her revelation. I was *sickened,* to be honest, and under the heaviness of my emotions I hung my head and whispered, "I have no *rights* in my relationship."

Sara and I spent the next few weeks talking about rights in relationships, where in one moment she would almost *desperately* try to explain what they were. Then in the next, she would try to teach me how to obtain them by saying, "Just do it, Tracy. If you want to go and do something that you want to do, just do it! *GO!*"

My response, however, was always the same. "But Erik will get *angry.*"

"Then *let* him get angry," she would say.

That, however, was easier said than done. Sara was asking me to buck a system that I was trained not to buck. She was asking me to break rules that were forbidden to break. Plus, she was missing the biggest issue. I was the one who had to live with Erik's wrath or rage. If I attempted to implement my newfound "rights" all Hell would break loose. I *knew* that because I had tried before to exercise my "rights"; and each time I got "big," Erik inevitably got "bigger." In case Sara did not get the memo, "letting Erik be angry" was much easier said than done.

My therapy with Sara carried on for several months where over that time I learned a lot *in theory* about normal relationships. The problem, however, was the concepts didn't make it past the counseling seat.

It was a frustrating time as during my sessions, I would be grounded and clear minded. My inner voice would be on purpose and by the end of the meeting, I *knew* what I needed to do when I got home. However, *when* I got home, all my therapy went out the door and upon seeing Erik, I would become weak and cowardly. His temper would flare, my brain would freeze, and we would be right back to the unhealthy dynamics just like before.

In hindsight, I learned a critical lesson about abuse recovery during that time. I learned that no matter how hard you try to heal, unless you are in a safe environment, it is all an act in vain.

MEMO FROM NORMAL LAND®

"Healing can only take place in a safe environment."

Safe Environments

If you are not familiar with the term "safe environment", a safe environment is a place where you are *surrounded* by the things you *need* in order to heal. It is a *protective* environment where you can *safely* learn new skills and tools to *express* and *be* yourself without being discounted, ignored or punished.

A safe environment is where you develop your emotional muscles and establish boundaries for your personal well-being. It is a place where through acts of self-discovery you find your first voice, and then with that self-awareness, you mid-wife yourself to healing.

But where could that safe place be for me? I couldn't leave Erik. As crazy as it sounds, I didn't *want* to leave Erik! *I only wanted the pain in our relationship to end.*

Plus, how would I survive? I knew how to keep myself afloat within the crazy walls of my house. But "out there?" Through the eyes of my broken self-esteem, the thought was overwhelming.

Then of course, there was the challenge with my job. I couldn't just quit. Financially, I had too much riding on the line.

And most important, where would I go? My family lived hours away, and Erik already told me if I left, and he *knew* where I was, he would get me. If I stayed in town, though, he would eventually *find* me, *and then what?*

It was a horrible cycle of useless options: On one side I was scared to leave because I didn't *know* what would happen to me out in the real world. On the other side, I was scared to stay for I feared what *might* happen to me if I did.

One Saturday afternoon, though, I reached my fork in the road, and things were about to change.

After months of failed pregnancy attempts, our doctor told us that our only hope of conception would be fertility treatment.

They say that just before you lose your life, parts of it flash before your eyes. In hindsight, I had a version of that phenomenon while driving to the pharmacy that afternoon: My life started to flash before my eyes.

I was driving to the drug store and suddenly at the stop light my mind's eye was bombarded with flashes of my reality: I saw the tens of thousands of dollars of credit-card debt. I saw the craziness of the alcoholism. I saw Erik's violent temper (that was only getting worse), and I saw "me" curled-up in a human ball in complete fear.

I saw the fisted hole "memorials" splattered on the various

walls in our house and the violent and traumatizing arguments that preluded them. I saw the too many public scenes of embarrassment that had become Erik's version of normal. And I even saw Erik, as a child, being held at knifepoint, by his father.

I saw Erik kicking the dogs and locking me out of the house for hours. I saw him recklessly driving his car and holding me hostage just for the sake of laughs. I saw his family during the holidays picking on children and humiliating anyone outside the clan, just because they could. And I saw the thousands of dollars of house payments gambled away without a second thought or concern how it would affect my security.

I saw my lost dreams all go down the drain; I saw how he broke my spirit and my body without a second glance. And I saw how he, without thought, would compromise our safety, or, as I looked at the fertility prescription in my hand, *the life of our future child*, with no remorse.

My life literally hit me in the face and with it, a moment of clarity. I realized it was one thing for me to expose myself to the fear and craziness; but to do it to an innocent child *would be entirely wrong.*

Memo from Normal Land: The job of a child is to *be* a child. And one thing I clearly understood at that moment was that this unborn child would *never* have that chance to enjoy just *being* a child.

I pulled my car to the side of the road, and I wept. I wept because I knew I could no longer do this to myself. And I wept because I feared *what* holding this boundary might mean.

That afternoon I returned to the house, and I begged Erik to go to counseling. He, of course, refused telling me that I was asking him to "put his *fucking* balls in a vice." He proclaimed he would *never* talk to a stranger about his life… *Ever*.

I told him I would have to leave if he didn't go for help with me. He said he didn't care.

In hindsight, I think he didn't believe I would have the courage to leave if there was no change. And to be quite honest, I didn't know if I would either.

14

The ABC's of Control

Journal Entry - May 15 (Year 5 in the Abuse)

"...Oh God, I can't think right now. I am numb. I have to pack my bags, but I can't. I am so scared. I am literally frozen with fear. I can't imagine leaving this place. I don't know any other place but here! But, if I stay I might not make it. Please, God, don't hate me for what I am about to do..."

It took four weeks for me to gain the courage to leave the house; primarily because I had no idea where to go. I had no extra money to rent a place on my own. I couldn't move in with a "friend" because *I didn't have any friends left.* I also couldn't go to my parents. Erik said if I did, he would *"come find me."* Plus, he threatened that my parents would "pay the price" if they interfered in our marriage.

The "come find me" statement was a new remark Erik started making since we had our conversation about me leaving. Anytime I would go to the stores, to work, or we would be apart from one another, he would say, "If you leave and don't come home, I'll come find your ass."

I wasn't sure if Erik was puffing his chest, or if he was serious, but one night around 4:00 a.m., I woke-up out of an uneasy sleep to find him towering over the end of the bed, silently watching me. It was an eerie moment. The night light in the room cast a silhouette around his body, and all I heard was the sound of his alcohol labored breathing.

I lay in bed pretending I was asleep and hoping he would just go away. But he didn't. In fact, for several minutes he stood over me and didn't move; nor did I.

Erik finally broke the suspended silence when in a slow yet direct voice he said, "Tracy. I am *not* going to let you leave."

My heart pounded in my chest, and he continued, "You hear me clearly. You are *my* wife and *my* wife only. No other man will ever have you because you *belong* to me."

He paused for another brief second, pointed his finger at my resting body and said, "I am not going to let you *fucking* leave." Then, as slowly as he appeared, he shut the light off behind him and disappeared from the room for the night.

Leaving

The next morning Erik departed for a three-day, out-of-state work conference and when we said goodbye, I didn't tell him I was leaving. Admittedly, I lied to Erik. I was too cowardly to tell him the truth, so instead I said I would be waiting for him when he returned.

You would think I would have jolted out the door moments after his plane departed. But if the truth is known, I didn't have the emotional strength to move. Not "move" as in go to another house. I mean "move" as in get off the couch. Anytime I thought about leaving, and more intimidating, when I thought about *what might happen after I left,* I would freeze in fear and retreat to my safety corner on my couch.

I don't know if it was emotional paralysis, or trauma, or fear, or Stockholm Syndrome, but whatever it was, I did *not* have the strength to walk out the door on my own. So after two days of fear-induced couch squatting, a co-worker stepped in, loaded my clothes into my car, and hand-walked me to my car.

MEMO FROM NORMAL LAND®

"Abuse is not always an easy thing to leave."

When I left Erik's house that day, I walked away from everything I owned. I packed my clothes, and my dog, Skitaka in my car, shut the door behind me and left. *Everything* that I had worked for over the four years, I left behind.

I decided not to take anything with me for *several* reasons. First, I knew Erik would be furious, and there would be a price to pay for leaving. But to have him return and also have *his* things missing as well? No way was I going to sign on for that ride.

My new home was an undisclosed location two and a half hours away from Palm Springs. A work friend of a friend gave me a room in her apartment which was located minutes from my corporate office in Newport Beach. It was a beautiful, small, but more important, private home where Erik would not be able to find me.

My new house was blissfully peaceful. But all of that changed two days later when Erik returned from his trip, found my closet empty, and Skitaka and, I gone. Unfortunately, the reality that I left, and the fact that *he had no control over it,* made him nuts.

Nuts to the point that I had over 40 missed calls from Erik that first night. He called until the wee hours of the morning, screaming and demanding to know *why* I took all of my clothes, *when* I was coming home, and most important, *where I was.* Erik was obsessed with finding where I lived.

I thought Erik's behavior was out of control that day. But I would soon discover that it was just the beginning of a new form of insanity with Erik.

Hour-after-hour turned into day-after-day where my phone would start ringing in the morning before I woke, and would not stop until the wee hours of the next morning when I slept. Each message was always the same. "Call me the *fuck* back, NOW!"

In the beginning, I "obeyed" Erik, and like a trained scared dog I would *immediately* return his calls, and then sit on the phone for hours while he berated and belittled me for leaving.

During that time people asked me why I didn't simply ignore his calls. For some reason, I couldn't. Even out of his presence Erik was able to control my life. Plus, I knew deep inside if Erik could reach me immediately by phone, it would keep him from wanting to *find* me in person.

I learned that lesson the hard way when after *not* returning Erik's calls, he started making unannounced drop-ins at my work.

I have to admit I didn't see that one coming. In the four years of our marriage, Erik *never* came to see me at my place of employment. My work site was 20 minutes from our house. As far as he was concerned, it was "20 minutes out of his way." So when he started making unexpected drop-ins, it was not only unnerving but more so embarrassing. Day-after-day he would storm into my office, make a public scene and refuse to leave until I physically saw him.

The cycle started to make me feel crazy: I would ask Erik not to call. He would continue to call. I would not return his calls. He would appear at my work site unannounced and say I had "forced him" to do it. I would tell him I did not want to see him and ask him to leave my worksite. He, in turn, would become emotional and confrontational in front of my coworkers and refuse to leave until I agreed to see him later. Just like old times, Erik would wear me out until I would say "yes" to end the chaos.

It was evident after I left that, "stone-faced Erik" was distraught and disjointed and as the cycle of abuse repeats itself, Erik was also once again *determined* to get me back. And *again* like the past, he did what I called his **ABCD's** of control.

A: **Attention:** For the first time in years, Erik showered me with attention and started doing *everything* I begged him to do for *years.* For example, he canceled his parents and sisters credit cards. He took vacation time and started coming home early, e*ven though I was no longer there.* He even started to attend the church I begged him to try for years.

When Erik realized that I was not budging as quickly as I had in the past, his aggressive attention suddenly turned into "caring attention", and *20 to 30 times a day* he called just to "see how I was." He filled my post office box with love letters and cards. And he even bought me a brand new diamond tennis bracelet *on a credit card he opened in my name,* no less.

When the Attention campaign didn't work, Erik went to plan **B: Bombardment.** That's when he got his family involved and one-by-one they called in tears, promising me there would be no more credit card abuse, name calling, or drunk and violent holidays. I believe they expected me to run back to Erik at the sound of their "good" news. I, however, responded by telling them, "Thank-you, but only time will tell."

Following his family bombardment, Erik then got the Wrecking Crew involved, who they systematically called and also begged me to return. They campaigned that Erik "had changed" and that he "saw the error of his ways." I, however, informed them that Erik could not *change* 30 years of behavior in just a few weeks, so we would have to wait and see.

Erik then got his *new* pastor involved, a man who met Erik only two weeks prior. The pastor called and with religious guilt told me that "Erik was a changed man." He advised me that as a "God-fearing woman" it was my responsibility to give Erik a second chance. I politely informed him that as an *Erik-fearing* woman, my answer was "no."

When I refused to respond to Erik's "loud" techniques, he pumped the bombardment campaign "louder", and went as far as to purchase a two-month *billboard* that proclaimed his love for to me. It was located *in front of my worksite, on Interstate 10 West.* The eye-sore was horrifically embarrassing.

When the Bombardment campaign didn't work, as a last ditch effort, Erik finally went to Plan *C:* **Counseling.**

There was however only one problem with this step. Erik

didn't go to counseling to get well or to work on us. Erik instead went to counseling (as he said) "to get me back." Erik's life was changing, and his comfort zone was gone. For the first time in years he felt out of control and according to him, he was determined to do whatever "he needed to do to get life back to normal."

I denied it at the time, but deep in my heart, I knew the truth behind his counseling maneuver. I knew that couple's therapy was only a way to get *me* home, so he could feel better. I knew our counseling had nothing to do with improving us. But none-the-less, with high hopes and oozing doses of denial, I gave it a try.

His counselor's name was Morgan. She was an attractive lady in her late forties who knew her stuff. She was an alcoholism expert who brought out charts and graphs and timelines that explained the progression of the nasty disease; which they all fit Erik, me and his family to a tee.

During our sessions, Morgan shared about "enabling" and "co-dependence." She outlined in no uncertain terms that Erik was a "co-dependent" and "dry alcoholic"; that his mother was an "enabler"; and undoubtedly his father was an addict. I remember Erik looking at me with amazement. I looked back at him with resentment.

And why wouldn't I? Here a perfect stranger was telling him something I had known for years. But because it came from her and not me, he, of course, believed it. It was one more example that showed what little respect Erik had for me.

During our counseling sessions, Morgan asked me to share honestly about my relationship with Erik. With fear and apprehension, I told her *some* of my secrets. This in turn made Erik uncomfortable, and angry.

To defend himself, Erik would attempt to turn the tables off him and onto me. Morgan however never let him get away with it. Whenever he started to shame me, she would stop him and say, "Erik, focus on you, not on Tracy. We will not Tracy-bash today."

Erik looked at her with amazement and disbelief. "I'm shaming her? I don't think that I am shaming her. I am only telling you the truth about her, and what she does."

"No Erik." She would try to explain. "You are *not* telling the truth. You are *shaming* her and piling unwarranted *guilt* on her. It is a form of control, and you *cannot* do it in here." Erik responded to her boundary with contempt. I just looked at the ground and smiled.

During our sessions with Morgan, we talked about a lot of different things within our relationship. We talked about the disease of alcoholism; about Erik's inability to disconnect from his parents; and about Erik's problem with needing to be in control at all times.

During our sessions, Morgan also talked to Erik about his "sex addiction" as she diagnosed it; which introduced Erik to the topic of intimacy. "Not sex, Erik – *Intimacy*" she tried to explain. "It is the non-sexual bonding moments in a relationship. It has nothing to do with sex. It has to do with *love and connection*." Erik had a difficult time grasping the concept.

I will never forget that particular session because Morgan handed me a blue sheet of paper listing 15 examples of intimacy. My eyes raced down the page desperately searching for one, *just one* example that our relationship reflected; but nothing. Not a single thing on that list described "us" as a couple, and with great disappointment, I hung my head and wept.

During our last sessions together the topic of Erik's treatment plan came into focus, and in that meeting we talked about how *if* Erik was going to get well, it was going to take years. We talked about how *if* he were going to get better, I would need to be "the strong one," "the one to help him through things," because *if* he were going to get well "it would not be easy on *him*."

The news was more than I could handle, and before I knew it my bottled-up, raw emotions and untamed anger uncorked, and I began to yell, "*Easy* on him?! Be *strong* for him?! What about *me*?! What about *my* needs!? What about *my* pain and *my* shame and *my* road to recovery?! I don't have the strength to be the strong one *now*. Two or three years ago, maybe even a year ago, I did. I begged and pleaded for him to get help, but *no*, he couldn't do it *then*. He had to wait until *now;* until *now*, when finally, *he* has something to lose! He had to wait until *now* when I'm all given out! Well, I don't have the *strength* to be there for him *now*. I was there for him for years, always being the *strong* one, *but having to pretend to be weak;* and now, *now* that I have *nothing* left inside, you still want *more*?! I'm holding onto dear life with every fiber of my being, and *now* you want *more* from me? For God's sake! What about *me! What* about ME!?"

Morgan pulled me out of the room to calm me down and after a few minutes she said, "Tracy, you need to be honest with me. Is there someone else in your life? Is there another person?"

I looked down at the floor as the tears dripped out of my eyes and thought about my life, about my future and the question she posed. *"Is there someone else?"*

I reflected on the last few weeks and thought about my newfound rights: I have the *right* to be happy. I have the *right* to pursue my dreams. I have the *right* to a standard of treatment. I have the *right* to have the spiritual beliefs of my choice. I have the *right* to live in peace. I have the *right* to get well. I have the *right* to *be* well.

I paused for a brief second, lifted my head and wiped the tears from my face. I took a deep breath and rolled over her question one more time. *"Is there another person?"*

I felt an internal shift in my soul and with it, I looked Morgan directly in the eye and rhetorically responded, "Is there another person?" I pulled my shoulders back and smiled a genuine smile of strength. "Yes Morgan, there is another person. That other person is *Me."*

15

D - Death: The Ultimate Form of Control

MEMO FROM NORMAL LAND®

*"If people can't respect my life,
it is up to me to respect it for myself."*

Erik didn't handle the news of me discontinuing our counseling sessions very well, and Morgan, understanding my fear of his temper insisted on telling him, herself. Lucky for me she stalled the news by ten minutes, so that I could get on the road.

I don't know what happened behind the closed doors of the counseling session, but I do know what happened on the other side. Erik's behavior intensified. His obsession to get me back escalated and in an attempt to gain control (once again), he switched to his final technique *of control*, Plan *D:* **Death.**

Erik's Death Plan started by first threatening *me* with death. He would leave haunting voicemail messages like, "You said until *death* do us part, *and I will hold you to it*." Or, "No other man will *ever* have you. You wait and see." Or "You are *my* wife; and *my* wife only."

As a sidebar, according to F.B.I. Reports, 70% of female homicides due to Domestic Violence happen *after* a woman leaves.

The reason is that abuse is about *control*, and when a woman leaves an abusive relationship, it takes the control *away* from the abuser; which in turn makes the violator feel out-of-control; who will then respond by taking new measures of abuse to regain the control they once had.

True to form, after I chose to stop seeing Erik altogether, was when the stalking began.

Erik started stalking me on my worksite where if he weren't *calling* my office dozens of times a day, he would be *lurking* in the parking lot at the end of my work day. If he weren't hiding in the parking lot, he would *bombard* his way into my office and disrupt anyone and anything that stood in his way. I truly started to feel like a hunted animal, looking over my shoulder with every step.

Unfortunately, Erik's constant disruption at my work site put my job in jeopardy, and it wasn't long until my bosses warned me that if I didn't "stop him," I would have to find new employment. *Of course,* I could not stop him, so in the midst of everything, I suddenly found myself jobless.

You would think *not* having Erik's daily harassment at work would have brought me some relief. But it wasn't long until Erik used his stalking skills to find the only safe heaven I had left, which was my home.

Erik found my undisclosed location by calling the bank. I made the mistake of opening an account at the same institution we used when we were married. He called the bank, pretended he was me and provided them with my contact details. He then informed them that he had moved, *yet had not received his new checks.* And they, *not thinking that Tracy was a female name,* handed my personal information, as well as my safety and peace to him on a silver platter.

Lucky for me, one of the Wrecking Crew wives called and warned me about Erik's discovery. Her husband was apparently talking with Erik after he found my home address. As she put it, "Erik was crazed." He said something to his friend about *"coming to get my ass and bring it home."* In the last communication we had, she informed me that Erik knew where I lived, and he was on his way to get me.

That night a friend of mine sat by the window with a baseball bat as I fearfully packed my clothes and my limited possessions. Then in the wee hours of the morning, I moved to a new undisclosed location and went into complete hiding. That was the day Erik's Plan D changed, and he began threatening to kill himself.

Journal Entry - July 4 (year 6 in the abuse)

"...I can't stand this pressure. What will I do if he really pulls the trigger? Should I go back to save his life? Or do I stay away, to save mine?"

When Erik's death threats shifted from me to him, his behavior took on new levels of insanity where every night he would leave messages on my machine, saying he had a gun to his head and would pull the trigger if I did *not* return his call, immediately. Needless to say with fragmented emotions and insurmountable guilt, I frantically called him back every night and begged him not to pull the trigger.

Night-after-night turned into week-after-week where Erik would threaten to take his life and where I would sit on the phone like a puppet, begging him not to do it.

Finally, on a July evening after weeks of the insane cycle *I* had a shift. There was no significant reason *why* I changed. I just did, and in a blink of an eye, I physically felt my body tell me I *could not* do this chaos anymore. I *could not* continue holding the responsibility of his life in my hands. I *could not* be a hostage to whether or not he wanted to live or die.

My mind, my body, my soul clearly told me that I had finally had *enough*; and in turn, I took a huge step of courage and made a difficult choice.

MEMO FROM NORMAL LAND®

"Your body will tell you when enough is ENOUGH."

Like every night prior, Erik (on queue) called me. Like every evening before, I (on queue) called him back. Then *again* as so many times before, I (on queue) painfully listened as he told me the gun was on his chin and he would pull the trigger if I did not come home.

Usually, at this stage of our pathetic production, my stomach would sink, *and* my eyes would fill with tears. But that night, *I* responded differently.

"Erik..." I said while steadying my voice. "The choice to live or die does not rest in my hands. It rests in yours. I cannot be responsible if you choose death. It will be your choice. So hear me clearly, Erik. *I do not want you to die.* I do not want you to pull the trigger. But the choice to live or to die is up to you. So I am going to hang up the phone now Erik, and call 9-1-1. I am sorry, but I cannot be hostage to this pain anymore."

I paused for a brief second; then I closed the phone, called 9-1-1, got on my knees and released Erik to the heavens with a prayer.

Two anguishing days passed with total radio silence from Erik and during that time, I thought for *sure* he had killed himself. I thought for *sure* to get back at me, he had pulled the trigger.

But my concerns were all in vain when three days after the 9-1-1 call, *Erik phoned*. And guess what? He was alive. Only now, rather than being the teary, suicide-talking Erik, he was the old, *angry* Erik; back from the emotional grave of self-pity and trying to start the insanity cycle once again.

I honestly could not wrap my brain around it. I thought leaving Erik would make my life better. I thought if I left "him" my problems would go with *him*. But as I stood on the cusp of the insanity cycle again, truth was telling me that *nothing* had really changed. My life was *still* in a state of chaos and pain. It was *still* spinning out of control with the insanity of abuse. And worse, this time, I could *not* blame Erik for any of my issues, because *I* was the one at the wheel, steering my life into yet another round of destruction.

Nerice

Her name was Nerice. She was a referred to me by Di, a fiery redhead I worked with at my previous job. For months, Di had nudged me to see Nerice, as supposedly she was a good therapist. And apparently (by the evidence of my life), I *desperately* needed one.

At the moment I met Nerice, I knew I had made the right decision. She was an educated lady in her mid-40's, an ordained minister, and a Marriage and Family and Child Counselor. She was loving and nonjudgmental, easy-going, yet firm at the same time. And to this day I will never forget the first words after our brief introduction. She said, "I just want you to know, I don't want to be seeing you in a year from now."

Nerice and I had a lot in common. She was a former model scout. I was in pageants. She was an ordained minister and counselor. *I sought God's direction and mental stability in my life.* She had survived a dysfunctional marriage and the disease of alcoholism. Alcoholism and dysfunction destroyed my life.

Meeting Nerice was like meeting a bright light. Shaking her hand was like shaking the hand of my guardian angel. She told me that day that as long as I wanted to get better, she was committed to helping me find my path to safety and happiness. *That was, as long as I was willing to walk the journey to get there.*

Part IV

Breaking Up with Abuse

The Ten Steps to Healing

The Courage to Say "No More"

16

Breaking Up with Abuse

MEMO FROM NORMAL LAND®

"Healing begins with me."

Journal Entry – August 15 (year 6)

"Sometimes I look at myself, and see an ice cube. It's as though my emotional development froze, and somehow I got stuck in a stage of adolescence. As I get well and begin to thaw, I find myself with the emotional tools of a child. No wonder I feel so frightened. I am literally an adult with the emotional skills-set of a child."

Healing was not easy. In fact, to this day, it still feels like the fight of *my life*. I guess that's because, in part, it was.

By the time I *re-entered* life, (as I refer my wake-up moment to) I had given so much of my personal power to Erik, that I literally had no idea how to manage myself anymore.

In our first session I described this emotional disconnect to Nerice by saying that I felt like a child in an adult's body. Or better stated, I felt like an adult with the skills and mindset of a child. She promptly confirmed that my personal assessment was almost on point. The years of abuse had left me with a condition called Emotionally Stunting. In general, this meant that the years of abuse traumatized me with a highly immature decision-making condition. As a result, just like a child who has limited life skills and abilities, my healing would require me to learn to talk, think and react in new ways that were foreign to me.

The Official Diagnosis

I was at my second session when Nerice officially gave my "pain" a name. She said I was suffering from something called the Abused Woman Syndrome. Which upon hearing her diagnosis, I immediately and defensively rejected.

"Me? Abused? No way" I challenged. I am not the *type* of woman who gets abused. I am a college graduate. I came from a good family. I worked in Corporate America. I believe in God! And don't forget, Erik *loved* me. How could someone who *loved* me, want to hurt me?"

Plus, Nerice missed the most discrediting piece of evidence to prove her case: Erik never *hit* me, so how could I be abused?

That afternoon I would learn my first lessons in abuse recovery. I learned that day that a person doesn't have to be physically violated to suffer from the Abused Woman Syndrome. I discovered that abuse isn't isolated to physical violence, alone. I became educated that abuse comes in many forms including financial, verbal, spiritual, sexual *and emotional* cruelties. I was enlightened that abuse in any of these forms could, and *will* cause the same emotional trauma as do bruises and broken bones; and I was set straight in truth by discovering that status, including religion, education, gender or upbringing doesn't protect a person from the destruction of abuse.

In no uncertain terms, that day Nerice confirmed I was, in fact, in an abusive relationship, and without a doubt, was suffering from the *Abused Woman Syndrome.*

My journey to wellness started that summer afternoon, and over the months that followed Nerice and I began what she called "Crises Counseling."

The entire process took place over a 24-month period where on a weekly basis she and I would untangle my issues, and and one-by-one, confront my emotional demons.

At the end of 2 year period, my journey unveiled ten key lessons that helped me overcome the pains and paralysis of abuse. They were ten lessons that helped restore my self-esteem. They were ten lessons that gave me back my emotional legs. And they were the ten lessons that empowered me to repair my broken emotional system from years of trauma.

Some could say that these ten lessons showed me a roadmap *out* of the world of abuse. I prefer to say these ten lessons gave me the power to *reclaim* my life.

NOTE FROM THE AUTHOR: Since the original writing of this book, Dr. Tracy has written a 20-part recovery program called "Reclaiming Me". For more information on the complete program, visit our website at www.DrTracy.tv

17

Session Is In

NERICE: *"How's that **denial** working out for you?"*

ME: *"**Denial**?" (I said as my face flushed and my eyes popped like a deer in headlights; because I was busted.)*

NERICE: *"Tracy, you need to learn to tell yourself the **truth**. Hiding behind **denial** will only keep you stuck."*

Session Is Out

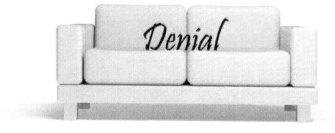

Step 1: Breaking up with Denial

Journal Entry September 3 (year 6 in the abuse)

"Last night I had a dream. I was standing shoulder-to-shoulder next to a man who was supposed to be my husband. In both our hands we carried shields.

From every direction, we were suddenly being assaulted by bullets. But like a team, he and I stood united; he, guarding my back when I needed it, and I guarding his when he needed it. From above I heard a voice (that, in my dream was God) that said, "This is a marriage problem - where the attack comes from the outside."

The next moment, I was once again standing shoulder-to-shoulder with my husband. Like before, in our hands we both carried shields. Like before from every direction bullets ambushed us. This time though when I turned my back toward my husband to shield him from bullets, rather than he protect me from the harm, he instead turned against me and attacked me from behind. From the heavens, I then heard a voice say, "This is a problem marriage - where the attack comes from the inside."

I was 15 minutes into my weekly session with Nerice, barely past the basic pleasantries, when she bluntly asked me about a verbal altercation between Erik and me earlier that week.

Out of habit, I went into Project Protection Mode, which meant first protecting Erik by making it look like a *less-than* incident;

then protecting *myself*, so that I didn't look like such a loser for taking his abuse, *again.*

Perfect and on queue, I proceeded to sugar coat and downplay the verbal assault to nothing more than an "ex-lovers misunderstanding."

Facing Denial

Professionals in every field of recovery agree that coming out of denial is one of the first steps in healing. They say in fact, that unless you're willing to take this initial step of recovery, healing might not be possible.

If *only*, it was that easy. I mean, who in their right mind wants to remove their rose-colored glasses, and face the ugliness of their life? Who wants to bring their emotional blind spot into focus and see the panoramic view of their horrific pain, shame, and failure?

Speaking for the millions of denial addicts, I can confidently say, "Not Me", and that is *precisely* why *for years* I held onto my denial; like a life jacket in a tsunami.

My Friend Called, Denial

Denial might seem like a negative word to some, or even complete stupidity to others. To those living in pain, however (especially to me in the midst of my chaos) denial was the furthest thing from "bad" or "negative" or "stupid."

In fact, in my world of dysfunction, Denial was actually my friend; not to mention my protector, my haven of refuge, my robe of comfort, and my Kool-Aid of choice that I gladly drank to survive my world of craziness.

With Denial by my side, I could put on a pageant smile during an embarrassing public scene, and I could cover-up a shameful moment with a "he doesn't really mean it" grin. My friend called Denial, empowered me to say "God is Good" when things were horrible. And best of all, my friend called Denial, allowed me to sprinkle *Magical Thinking* over anything that was beyond my control to change.

If you are not familiar with the term Magical Thinking, it's a denial survival tool we abuse victims use to convince our self that things can, and will, *magically* change. Meaning, it's our "I Dream of Genie" blink-of-the-eye *false* belief system; where we think we can *magically* "love" our abuser into happiness. Or it's where we *fantasize* that with the next paycheck, prayer or promotion, life will *magically* get better. Or, it's where we believe that one day he will *magically* wake-up and be something new; like "kind", for example.

Living in denial was my emotional skin. It was *how* I protected myself. So when Nerice said I needed to *shed* my denial to heal, I couldn't help but passionately resist.

To me, Nerice was asking me to release any source of control I had in a world that was spinning out of control. Or more metaphorically speaking, I felt she was advising me to walk away from the emotional Leaning Tower of Pisa I had been *shouldering* for years.

Though well-meaning counsel I'm sure, all I heard was, "Gee *Trace*, even though your entire life will come crashing down, I need you to trust that somehow; in spite of the ruins, it will all be okay."

MEMO FROM NORMAL LAND®

"Mosaics are built from shattered pieces."

Seriously though, how could "it" be okay? I had built my entire world on the lies of denial. Tossing even *one* of them would set a domino effect of pain, *and life change* in uncontrollable motion.

If I faced my reality I would then have to accept that the man I would have *died* for, was in truth, the man who hurt me most.

Which if I accepted that fact, I would then have to face that my husband, *not a stranger*, but my *husband* was abusive; which that reality would mean I could *no longer* make excuses (like too much alcohol or stress overload) for his wrong behavior. Which *that* would mean, I would *have* to hold him accountable for his actions, which I must point out, I had no idea *how* to do.

Facing my reality would mean accepting that Erik's actions were *intentional acts of harm*. In other words, Erik abused me because he *could*. And if this were the case, that meant that perhaps Erik never *really* loved *me* in the first place. Which that would conclude that all I did for "love"; all I gave for "love"; all I lost for "love" (including my dignity, my house, my furniture, my job, and my car, which I had to sell to pay credit card bills that I got stuck with in the divorce) was never done for "love" in the first place. And if not done for love, what was it?

On top of that ugly mess, there was also the reality of what I had personally become while in the abuse, which if I took off my rose-colored martyr glasses, *was a big fat zero*.

I had abandoned my whole life for Erik; my Dreams, my Career, my Purpose. my Self-esteem. I lost grip on nearly *everything!* My *entire* focus had become managing Erik's anger, and reality check 001: There were *not* a lot of high-paying jobs, if *any*, that listed "good at managing Narcissistic adult temper tantrums" as a pre-requisite for employment.

Am I Stupid?

I know people tend to label women like me as a "glutton for punishment," a "professional victim" or my personal favorite "stupid." But one thing healing has taught me is that denial-based survivorship is anything but *stupid*.

I say that because behind the blank stare we publicly display in the midst of the chaos, we Denial Addicts *know* what's going on around us. Meaning we *know* that the drinker is drinking, the abuser is abusing, and the gambler is gambling. Deep inside we *are aware* the liar is lying, the player is playing, and the doper is doping.

When push comes to shove, we are completely aware of what's unfolding in front of our eyes, and we know most *every time* it unfolds.

The problem, however, is that our situation is so vast and intimidating to us, that just like the startled deer in oncoming headlights, the overwhelmingly causes us to freeze.

Popular belief wants to say we freeze out of stupidity. That, however, is not the case at all. The reality of our situation is that we freeze because we are in complete fear. Meaning, we freeze because we have *no idea* how to stop the train that's coming directly at us. We freeze because we have *no clue* how to fix the monster that is eating us alive. We freeze because we have no idea how to *defend* ourselves against this tidal wave of chaos that is drowning us.

The truth is that we have *no* answers on how to solve our gigantic problem. So, in the attempt to not *die* (or better stated, in the effort to survive) we instead *partner* with denial. We put on its rose-colored glasses. We paint false silver linings of hope, we force our self to go numb, and then we pray *beyond all reason and logic* that *"it"* (our monster, our crisis, our tidal wave) will eventually pass.

But trust me when I say, *"it"* will not pass by using denial as our tool of hope. In fact, it *cannot* pass if we continue to use denial as our tool of change.

The reason (it *cannot* pass) is because *denial is not a tool.* In fact, denial is nothing more than a ghost life-jacket that will eventually weight us down and leave us to drown.

I compare living in denial to being on a raft boat in the open waters of the sea; *with an approaching typhoon, no less.* Sure, that temporary raft of denial might initially keep us afloat. But when the winds and storms of life happen (and believe me, abuse comes with a lot of wind and storms) that little boat of denial will not be able to keep us safe. Under the extreme pressures of the crisis, the raft boat of denial *will* eventually form holes. And when it does, it will start to sink; and sadly, it will not think twice about taking you down with it.

Breaking Up with Denial

I know how frightening it is to think about *breaking up, or ending* your relationship with denial. I know how blinding it feels to consider removing our rose-colored glasses, or to stop drinking the magic potion that keeps us somewhat blurred.

I know how intimidating it is to soberly face the experiences we survived; and sometimes worse, to accept what we have become in light of them.

It goes without question that stepping out of denial *is* nothing short of frightening. However, *if* we are going to heal; or if we are going to stop the cycle that's killing us; or if we're going be free from the memories that haunt us, we *must* be willing to wake-up out of denial and step into our *today*.

OMG, It Sucks

It's important to note that stepping out of denial and into reality doesn't mean we will like what we see. In fact, we will probably dislike 95% of our discovery.

It also doesn't mean our entire life plan will suddenly fall into place. Our what, when and how will only be unveiled during the unfolding and self-discovery process.

What stepping into reality will do is give us the gift of solid ground. It will empower us with *emotional clarity,* by putting *truth* into our viewfinder. Truth, which you will find as you enter into recovery, *is* the first step of healing.

In fact, it is the main ingredient required to start the journey to reclaiming our soul. That's probably why both Buddha and the Bible claim that "The truth will set us free." When it comes to repairing our life and winning the battle against abuse, reclaiming the lost land of truth is the mandatory first line of defense to sanity. It is the strategic prescription we need to heal from the trauma and memories of abuse. And all we have to do is accept, without judgement, what *is*. It is called our Truth. It is our first step to healing. And it is our roadmap to being set free from the pains and trauma of abuse.

MEMO FROM NORMAL LAND®

"You will know the truth, and your truth will set you free."

18

Session Is In

ME: "I **have** to do that."

NERICE: "Who said?

ME: (Blank stare and no response.)

NERICE: "And more importantly, who gave them the **right** to have the final say on what is best for your life?"

Session Is Out

Step 2: Breaking-Up with Rules

There are many heroes in the World of Recovery. One of those significant contributors is the late Elizabeth Kubler-Ross, who created the most recognized module for grief recovery called "The 5 Stages of Grief." In her grief recovery module, Ms. Kubler-Ross identified the natural cycle of emotions a person processes through whenever we experience trauma or loss. The five stages of grieving include:

(1) Denial

(2) Bargaining (the would've and should've)

(3) Depression

(4) Anger

(5) Acceptance

You would think with my storage House of Wounds, I would have easily merged into the grieving cycle of healing. It was a few steps outside of my denial, and what was supposed to be on the cusp of my *natural* grieving process, where I hit my first block in recovery: It was time for me to start *feeling* the emotions of grief. However, due to my trauma, I literally could *not* allow myself *to* grieve.

Don't get me wrong. It's not that I had lost the ability to mourn and grieve. It's not that I resisted the concept. On all levels, I wanted and was ready to grieve.

I, however, could not bring myself *to* grieve because, at the core of my being, I didn't believe I had the *right* to grieve.

In fact, I *feared* the concept of grieving because to me, grieving meant making "noise" (as Erik called my outward expressions of emotion). Grieving meant talking or crying. It meant sharing and expressing. And all of these outward emotions "broke" Erik's rules; which ultimately meant punishment.

I was sitting in Nerice's office sharing my block of confusion when in almost a mind-reading way she gently said, "Tracy, I give you permission to grieve. But, it will first require you to **break** Erik's rules."

Journal Entry October 13 (year 6)

"...I am a college graduate and a corporate executive. However, if I look at myself with truth-telling eyes, I am actually someone who has lived according to everyone else's rules. Everyone's that is, except mine.

It seems that every part of me (my job, my relationship, and even my religion) I have lived according to everyone else's expectations; according to what everyone else thought was best for my life; according to what they told me I should do, or what I should believe. I have unfortunately lived my life according to everyone else's rules. That is, everyone's except mine..."

Life Rules

Just before my thirtieth birthday, I had to embrace an ugly truth about myself. That truth or "reality" was that in spite of my college degrees and personal life accomplishments, I didn't know "Me." Meaning, I was a person who didn't know who I was unless someone told me who I was. I didn't know what I represented unless someone told me what I represented. I didn't even know what I believed (on a spiritual level) unless someone was telling me what I should believe.

My truth and reality were that I had lived my entire adult life according to the rules of everyone else. And in doing so, I stopped myself from becoming the only person I was ever meant to be, *which was the Authentic Me.*

MEMO FROM NORMAL LAND®

"Rules are meant to be broken."

The Creation of a *Personal Rule Book*

Nerice called the task the *"Personal Rule Book"* Project. If you're not familiar with a Personal Rule Book, don't feel bad. By my personal state-of-disaster, I obviously had no idea what one was, either.

For the record, a *Personal Rule Book* is an *intimate* list of rules we set for our self that establishes what we will accept, and what we will *not* accept, in life, our self, and others.

As an adult, a *Personal Rule Book* is a *tool* we *need* in our Life Tool Box to properly manage *Self,* so that love and life, work. And Memo from Normal Land: Without a Personal Rule Book, our life, and our relationships will become unmanageable.

Creating My Rule Book

The creation of my Personal Rule Book consisted of two specific tasks. The first project was to excavate or remove the "other" infused (i.e. Erik imbedded) rules that saturated my personal pages.

In the world of Manifesting, this step is known as the Vacuum Law of Prosperity, which basically is a space creating exercise that eliminates the bad, (or the no longer useful) in order to make room for the good.

I have to admit, part one of the Personal Rule Book project initially intimidated me. It was as though the ghost of Erik still had the power to haunt me from beyond our marriage grave. I honestly *feared* that if I went against Erik's "Law", he could somehow harm me for breaking his rules. Clearly, the post trauma effects of abuse emotionally, run deep.

It took some time, but one day, it appeared the heavens and the earth, the moon and the stars, *and* my relentless passion to heal finally all aligned, and for whatever reason, I awoke one morning and had what I call a "take back my life moment." With it, I did something long overdue, which was to bravely and unapologetically *break-up with Erik's rules!* (Hear the crowd roar loudly).

I have to confess this step of independence was immediately *life-changing.* No words can describe what it was like to openly express *my* feelings *and not be punished, or ridiculed for them.* Or to laugh at jokes without getting a threatening glare. Or to do certain things like *smile* at people in the grocery store, or for that matter, buy *whatever* I wanted in the grocery store; without getting harassed or yelled at *for hours* for doing it "wrong."

I can't tell you how incredible it was to talk on the phone to *anyone* I wanted, *whenever* I wanted, and about *whatever* I wanted; *and* to do it without getting a negative report card, or be on the receiving end of the three-day silent treatment. Without a doubt, breaking Erik's rules and finding my first voice, for the first time, was nothing short of spectacular.

I was told many times during my years of abuse that the grass was *not* always greener on the other side of divorce. Many people cautioned me (in the name of God) to "not hastily throw away my marriage." But now, having lived in both pastures and tasted the fruits of both fields, I can confidently say that when it comes to being free from someone else's rules, the grass is *very much greener* than are the pastures of control. Life *is* much more colorful *and much healthier* when we become the first opinion on what is right or wrong for our life.

Phase 2 - Writing Your Personal Rule Book

I spent several months breaking and erasing Erik's rules and influences from my Personal Rule Book. Which these ground breaking steps eventually led me to phase two of the Personal Rule

Book Project: It was time to create a set of personal rules of my own. However, I had *no* desire.

The concept of reverting to a life governed by "rules" did *not* set well with me. In my perspective, I had only recently escaped from Rule Bondage Land. I was still healing from the emotional shackles that denied me of my rights, power, expression and liberty. Yet now I was expected to re-enter a lifestyle *governed* by rules? My answer was unequivocally, "no." And in complete rebellion, I took *the path of total freedom* and refused.

I reference that part of my journey as my emotional commando days; and let me tell you, that pendulum swung to areas I still blush to admit. My father explained it best when in his Oklahoma accent he would say, "Honey, the further you pull back on that rubber band, the farther that darn thing is gonna' fly." And fly I did, all the way to the extreme opposite of who I once was with Erik.

My "rebellious rule" stage initially manifested itself in benign things like not making my bed, or refusing to cook *for three years;* all the way to more colorful and less PG-rated events that at the writing of this book went *in* The Vault, (and will *stay* in The Vault) forever.

I don't allow myself to reflect on my emotional commando days with negative self-judgement or regret. I knew I would eventually put my big girl panties on, and create structure and order for myself. I also knew that during that extreme pendulum swinging season, the freedom of *not* doing things *just because I could* was quite healing for my soul.

The pendulum of extreme eventually found its way back to a common sense, middle ground, and with it, my journey to writing my Personal Rule Book began.

My road to healthy structure was grounded in a self-awareness question, that asked, "why or who?" For example, I asked myself *"why* do I believe this"; *"who* told me this was truth", and *"who* said this was the best way for me?" Then, through investigation, as well as body, mind and soul feedback, I determined what path was *best* for *me*, based on what *felt right,* to Me.

Over the months that followed, I eliminated any belief or rule that was accompanied by someone else's *should or have to, and* then replaced those negative influences with a standard or guideline that was an *"I could,* or "want to", instead. Happily, as the months passed, there was a noticeable shift: The once empty shell of a woman started to be filled with beliefs and opinions of my own, that were courageously discovered and implemented on my own.

At the end of my Personal Rule Book Project, I learned three valuable lessons about the importance of rules.

First, I learned that rules come in only two forms: Good Rules and Bad Rules, and the only one's right for me are the ones that feel good to me. Second, I discovered that there's only one set of rules I'm to live by, which are those I write myself. Third, I learned that as we are ever-evolving beings, the rules that govern our life must be written in pencil. The reason is because, as we expand, some rules will stop working for us, which then we have the responsibility to cancel, re-write or replace them as needed.

I wrote my original Personal Rule Book over 20 years ago, and though today the number of entries might increase or decrease within the cycle of life, the very first entries I created consisted of 12 simple rules that I continue to honor to this day.

The 12 original entries that still headline my Personal Rule Book are:

1) I have the right to be happy.
2) If someone hurts me, I have the right to be mad, and appropriately protect myself.
3) I have the right to express emotion in healthy ways.
4) I have the right to say "no" without punishment.
5) I have the right to make mistakes.
6) I have the right to love.
7) I have the right to be loved.
8) I have the right to be selective when it comes to choosing my friends and loved ones.
9) It is good for me to give to people, but not to the point that I am given out.
10) I have the right to take care of my needs first.
11) It is my responsibility to keep myself safe.
12) I have the right and responsibility to become my personal best, without apology.

19

Session is In

NERICE: *"What's wrong?"*

ME: *"I think I won't **ever** love anyone like I loved him!"*

NERICE: (*Raising her hands as though she were having a Hallelujah moment*) *"Thank GOD Tracy! You can't afford it!"*

Session is Out

Step 3: Breaking-Up with the Addiction

Journal Entry, April 10 (year 6 in the abuse)

"It's a radical roller coaster some call, love. No one intentionally gets on, but once you are, it's like an addictive drug that's life-giving and life-taking; all in one. Its highs don't compare to anything that you've experienced, yet its lows run so deep, no blackness can describe. It makes you feel alive and dead; pumped-up and persecuted all in one. The Hellish roller coaster ride called love..."

I couldn't believe it myself. I had been away from Erik for several months. Then suddenly, after everything I went through; after everything it took to rebuild my life; *in spite of knowing how horrible Erik was for me*, I was actually having thoughts of going back to him.

Back to *Him?!* What the *\$*)@ was wrong with me? This guy had taken me to death's doors and dumped me there. I was *still* fighting to get back my life. And yet *now* I was questioning *if I could have done more to make it work?*

Was I a glutton for punishment? Was I a martyr for pain? "Maybe I'm just flat out insane?" I thought to myself. *Why*, when every warning sign screamed, "No! Stop! Don't do it!" was I contemplating going back for more?!

Nerice interrupted my crazy mind race. "Tracy, you have a condition."

"A *condition*?" I said through my emotional blur.

"Yes. A *condition*. It's called *LOVE* Addiction."

"I have a *WHAT* addiction?"

"You have a *LOVE* Addiction."

I couldn't believe my ears. Was Nerice saying the words *"Love"* Addiction? Meaning, was she telling me that this thing called *Love*, turned me into an *addict*? And was she saying that due to this "addiction" of mine, *I*, in the name of "love" had a part in destroying my life?

My answer and discovery that day was unfortunately, "Yes." My world had blown out of control, not just because of Erik and his abuse; but more so, my world was on the cusp of complete destruction because I had become an *addict:* An unaware, super junked-up, jonesing out-of-control, addict.

Is it Real?

Of all the reality checks along my road to healing, one of my most difficult "moments in the mirror" was accepting my addiction.

You see, I had always prided myself on being the goodie-two-shoes type. The holier-than-thou arrogant who looked down her nose at screwed-up people and said, "...that kind of stuff doesn't happen to *me*."

As karma would have it though, it did happen to me, and there I was, looking my reality in the face; learning to *accept* that I had become a junkie. A junkie, may I add, who unlike *normal* addicts who get addicted to things like alcohol or pills, had to find the path of complete *weirdness,* and make my drug of awkward choice, *a human being.*

Can you say baby barf moment? I could barely understand how a person got hooked on a substance. Yet, I chose a *human* dependency as my drug of choice? The thought repulsed me. The idea completely *confused me.* But more so, the concept made no sense to me.

Until that is, the day I discovered *how* and why addictions are formed. In hindsight I could have *never* avoided this bulls-eyed encounter. The pot-holes from my childhood laid me directly in the path of its destruction.

Addictions

Addictions are caused when those of us in deep emotional pain try to *solve* our aches by indulging in "something" to create *relief.* Some people try to anesthetize in alcohol or drugs; some with food and others with religion, to name a few.

As a Love Addict, apparently, my drug of choice was "love"; love that unfortunately came in a *human* form.

I guess on a note of self-empathy, becoming addicted to *love* is much better than being addicted to eating couch foam, per say. But then again, if I were addicted to couch foam, I would have probably recognized the wrongness of my issue much earlier.

The Hole in My Soul

Experts say that the deep emotional pain of Love Addiction stems from an intense *need to be loved* due to an extreme form of rejection or abandonment experienced in childhood.

When I learned that insight, I took a big "Ah-ha" breath, because I told Nerice on several occasions that since my childhood, I felt that I had a *hole in my soul*. I described it to her as "this ginormous hole in my soul that ran so deep, so internal, that I couldn't tell where it ended (if in fact, it ever did) or where it began."

I shared with her that I didn't know if any other person felt this internal hole. Real or not, it was there, inside of me. In fact, that hole was *always* there, deep inside of me, aching within my heart, weighting down my soul, and screaming to the Universe my ugly questions of shame: "Why doesn't anyone love me? Why am I so difficult to love? *Why can't somebody, just please, please, love me?!*"

The Internal Conflict with Love

It is a sociological and biological fact that we humans *all* need and want love. We are not created as asexual, stand-alone beings. Instead, as a member of the human race, we are designed by nature to bond, to feel grounded, to be connected, and yet fully expanded when infused with the emotion of "love."

That, however (and unfortunately) is *not* what "love" feels like to a Love Addict, at all. When we, Love Addicts fall in love, we experience bond*age*, rather than bonding. We become confused rather than grounded. And when we fall in love, we don't find the expansion of one Self. Love to us ,is the *extinction* of one's Self.

When we Love Addicts, fall "in love", we don't fall into it and find our wings. We Love Addicts instead, fall in love and eventually, completely *fall apart*.

Why We Stay

A common question or better stated, a collective *judgment* asked of a Love Addict is "Why do we stay?" I answer that question by sharing that, research shows that the number one fear in adults is public speaking. However, that fact does not apply to a *Love Addict.*

Recovery research shows that the number one fear of a Love Addict is the fear of *rejection* and *abandonment.* And *everything* we do, or we tolerate, or we accept, or live in denial of, or more specific, *why we stay,* is all in the attempt to *avoid* rejection, and its horrific counterpart, *abandonment.*

Meaning, we *stay* because deep within our soul, we believe if we survive the abuse and somehow stop the cycle (this time), it means the rejection of the violence didn't really happen. So we *stay* hoping our resilience proves to our soul that we're not so easily discarded and unloved.

We *stay* to silence the stinging love-abandoned questions that scream, "Why can't somebody just love me?!" or "Why am I so difficult to love!?" We *stay* as our way of shouting back, "I will not allow this to happen to me again!"

We *stay* because deep inside we, unfortunately, believe that we *are* unlovable or underserving of love. Our childhood abandonment trauma plays that message on repeat every day. So we stay because at a brain-washed level, it makes *sense* for us *to* stay.

The best comparison I can make is to say that we are like a starving child who is willing to eat garbage out of the trash barrel just to stay alive. We know at first bite it might be bad. But over time, the stench of *abusive love* actually smells good to our hungry, love-starved soul. So because of that unhealed and confused trauma wound, we *stay*.

We stay long after the passion has turned into pissed-off; the adoration has turned into only temporary acceptance, and the love that once gave us wings has turned into the machete that cuts off our emotional limbs.

To answer the question *"why"* we stay, we *stay* because love and abuse have somehow merged into one. We stay because now it all feels like "love," to us. We *stay* because at the end of the day we Love Addicts are *desperate* for love, and desperate people will do desperate things...like stay.

MEMO FROM NORMAL LAND®

"Desperate love is never a good form of love."

The Drug of Love

The worst part of our addiction is even when we recognize our mistreatment, we *don't* walk away. For reasons that even elude us, we *can't* walk away. *"Why can't we walk away?"* we internally scream.

We can't walk away because unfortunately, this "condition" or this *addiction* of ours, has literally gone toxic. It has migrated from an emotional addiction, to a *chemical* addiction. And guess what?! Our abuser is our poisonous love-dangling, *drug dealer*.

That's right, our *Dealer*. Our *Human Needle*. Our *Drug Lord of Love* who via the *drama and the trauma* in our relationship, hits us up with a substance called *Adrenaline*.

It's one of the most powerful and addictive chemicals *not* made on the streets. Instead, this euphoric producing substance is created inside our bodies. It has the potency *and seduction* of morphine. It is a pain reliever and energy booster in one, and the second we get it, the more we want.

So why can't we leave the abuse? We *cannot* leave because without us knowing it, we've now become hostage to our abuser's drama based adrenaline drip. It's a drip where with one glare; he can abandon us into deep lows, and then with one smile, accepts us, into ecstasy highs. It's a drip where he controls our supply, our dosage, and eventually our life, with every administered injection of passion or *rejection.*

When the drip stops (either when we leave the relationship, or when there's too much *calm* in the relationship) like any junkie, we slip into *withdrawal*. We can't sleep. We can't eat. Our brain goes into obsessive over-load with him, him, him, him, HIM!! Our heart pants, our mind races and then the lies of the addiction begin: "Just one more time, and I'll get it right" it shouts from our abandoned soul.

It's the combination of *that* toxic message; plus the fear of abandonment and rejection; *plus* our physical withdrawal from the adrenaline that sends us over the edge. And unfortunately, in our blurry, strung-out state, all we know is that our abuser, who is now both our Satan and Savior; can make it *all* go away.

So *without* our dignity intact, and against all logic and reason, we run back to our source and supply. We run *back* to that place where we feel both powerful and powerless; back to that place we can't seem to leave (nor can we understand why we stay). We run back to that place to silence our soul and get our fix, and as much as it dismays us, we run back to the cycle of abuse, again.

How We Got Here

It is important to know that Love Addicts are not born so abhorrently pitiful. In our defense, we became this pathetic-partner in love because somewhere in our past, most probably in our childhood, someone did something, or *neglected* to do something; which branded our soul with a horrific message. It's a trauma based message that says "I am not lovable."

Poor us. We have gone through life with one of the most painful messages a human can experience: Questioning if we are worthy of love. It's no wonder we seem so fragile and scared. The truth is, we are.

Healing

When Nerice first told me I had a Love Addiction, I have to confess, I felt *very* overwhelmed. I had so many questions, such as "Can love actually be an addiction? Is it really possible to be addicted to a person? If "yes", does that mean I have to stay away from people for the rest of my life?"

It seemed so unfair. Alcoholics don't need to learn how to drink socially to heal. Drug addicts don't need to learn to use meth *in moderation* to get through life. They need to *stay away* from their drug of choice altogether *if they want to live.*

What then, as a Love Addict was I to do? Was I going to have to "give-up" people and be alone forever? I didn't *want* to be alone for the rest of my life. Love is something we all need and deserve, don't we? But to heal, was I going to have to disconnect from the human race because people got me high?

Luckily the answer I discovered was, "No." Love Addicts don't have to be alone to in order to heal, because Love Addicts are not actually addicted to *people*, per se. Instead, we Love Addicts, are addicted to the *hope* of love that a *particular* type of person dangles in front of us: A person (May I add) who represents the original wound, and the original abandonment that punctured our soul in the first place.

The good news is that we adult Love Addicts are *not* whores for love. Instead, we Love Addicts are nothing more than a dented soul who is trying to fix a childhood wound; via our current day chaos. In other words, we are just little girls in adult bodies who are desperately (and tragically) trying to fill a gaping childhood hole in our soul. A hole that says, "Would somebody please love me." A hole that shouts, "I just want to be loved." A hole that we unfairly received when a primary person in our childhood dropped the "Love Ball" and created something we were too young to understand. Not to mention, too young to fix.

As a Love Addict, we can certainly try to deny we have a hole in our soul and pretend that the way we choose love will be different "the next time." But if we make that choice, there is one thing I can promise: We *will* become a Love Junkie. Meaning, as long as we deny that hole in our soul is there, we *will* continue to crash into our Human Needle(s) with the hope of hearing we are loved. We *will* continue to run back to our abuser and repeat the cycle of pain, again. And we *will* continue to go back for more. Even if he or she mistreats us; even if we wonder what the Hell is wrong with us; even if every fiber of our being screams, "No! STOP! Don't go!"

Unless we accept that we have a condition called Love Addiction; unless we face that we have *lack*-of-love issues (and then pro-actively heal from the *original* abandonment that we experienced). Unless we make the choice to detox and heal our self-love pain, we *will* repeat our cycle again. And one thing is guaranteed with this condition of ours, unless we make the choice to heal, we *will* go back for more.

20

Session Is In

Nerice: *"How are you feeling?"*

ME: *"Depressed."*

NERICE: *"How long have you been feeling depressed?"*

ME: *"I think forever..."*

NERICE: *"What does it feel like?"*

ME: *"It makes me **tired**...."*

(A long thought-filled pause lingers in the room.)

NERICE: *"Well then Tracy, why don't you just **stop** doing the things that make you so tired?"*

Session is Out

Step 4: Breaking Up with Depression

Journal Entry April 13 (year 7)

"I sometimes wish I could dunk my soul like silver and have all my emotional tarnish disappear..."

We were a few minutes into our weekly session when Nerice brought to the surface something I had known for years.

"Tracy," she said. "You're depressed."

The news wasn't earth shattering to me. It didn't take a brain surgeon to look at my eyes, my skin, and my demeanor to see the stench of depression swamping off me. My inner light had dimmed years ago. Or had it never fully been illuminated in the first place? Either way, I had just gotten used to living in its darkness.

"...And?" I blandly responded.

"*And* depression is not supposed to be a year-round staple in your emotional wardrobe. It is to be a seasonal piece that we experience during times of challenge or loss."

I looked at her with an, "I don't know what to do with that" expression. Taking my lead, she continued.

"We have two options for your healing. Option one is to go on an anti-depressant and treat your depression as Chemical Depression."

Nerice then explained that Chemical Depression is where our body's mood-related chemicals (such as serotonin, norepinephrine, and dopamine) dip, and the imbalance manifests itself in the feelings of *depression*.

She continued. "We can treat your depression with medication and soon you will start to feel better. *Or…*"

"Or what?", I asked.

"Or a second option is that we can treat you for *Situational* Depression."

I paused at the sound of her words. "*Situational* Depression, what's that?"

"In general, Situational Depression is when the *situation* you are in causes you to be depressed."

An overextended pause filled the room because I was having what I call an "Ah-Ha-Are-You-*F'ING*-Kidding-Me-DUUH-Download moment!"

If Situational Depression is caused by living in *situations* that make a person depressed, then my *situation* with Erik *was* a real-life IV drip of doom; where every morning I was administered a dose of depression with his disapproving face. And every night I was given my drip via his list of "you failed me" reminders. It was no wonder I suffered from depression for years. The *situation* I was in, literally made me depressed.

Disclaimer

I want to go on record and say that I am not against anti-depressants. Medication is an excellent source of treatment for depression. Therefore, if you are on anti-depressant medication, my recommendation is to stay on it. Anti-depressants are not a substance you can abruptly discontinue, as doing so without consulting your medical doctor can be vitally threatening.

That said, though, I *immediately* knew that *not* taking medication was the best path for me. Something innately told me that the root of my darkness *was* connected to "the situation" I was in (and in and in) and logically, I understood *if* I could learn to create better *situations* for myself, I could then relocate my emotions to a more joy-filled address.

MEMO FROM NORMAL LAND®

"Joy has an address."

But First, The Thug called Depression

In India, there is a word used to describe a murderer who kills their victims via strangulation. They call the person who commits that crime a "Thug".

I mention that because depression has been described as many things over the years. Doctors call it, mental illness. Spiritualist, call it a thinking disorder. The religious, call it a demon. I personally, however, give it the name, "Thug". Something that attacks us without warning, ransacks our thoughts, blackens our perspective; and then if that is not enough, grabs us by the emotional neck and slowly squeezes the breath, life and *light* out of us.

If you have never suffered from depression, I would enviously say "Congratulations."

If you *have* suffered, you can appreciate then, when I say

that getting out of its grips can feel like the fight of your life. At least it was for me, and, according to the CDC 2015 report on Depression, for 1 in 10 women in the U.S.A., as well.

The Wrong Prescription for Depression

If you've ever been on the receiving end of a non-depressant, there is one blaring *obvious*: Those who've never suffered from the dark side tend to believe our battle with depression is somehow a deliberate choice of misery.

Countless times I've heard non-sufferers attempt to "help" the sufferer, by unintentionally giving insensitive advice such as, "turn your frown upside down." Or, "just try to see the glass half full." Or my personal favorite", "why not pray a little more earnestly?"

I must say, in their proper place, I do believe that methods such as praying or positive thinking can and do serve a purpose in *maintaining* certain levels of Joy. But truthfully speaking, these morsels of guidance are by no means the required *prescription* to initially *stop* the depression, itself.

Due to its internal nature, depression is unfortunately not something we can "heal" by simply flipping our frown upside down, or by trying to seeing the at the end of the dark tunnel. It is also not something we can willingly "snap out of", nor can we "cure it" by prayer alone.

Instead, Depression, especially Situational Depression, requires us to bravely go deeper into our pain and discover *what* is launching our blues at the root level. In other words, it is investigating *why* our smile turned into a frown; or *how* we ended-up in the dark tunnel in the first place.

To heal from depression, we need to understand *why* the glass is empty; *what* the normal allocation healthy adults have in their glass, and most importantly, we need to discover *where* our personal *power* resides, so we can replenish our supply; if and when it gets depleted.

In order for us to overcome Depression, it requires us to pinpoint what I call the "Power Stealers" that drain us of our joy, and then with this enlightenment, begin to take the necessary steps that lead us to healing.

Power Stealers

There is a story in the New Testament of the Bible where Jesus of Nazareth was walking in a large crowd, and an ill woman approached him for healing. According to the story, the afflicted woman believed if she touched Jesus' cloth, she could be healed. As the story goes, the woman, who was surrounded by the masses, pushed her way through the crowd, reached out with perseverance and belief; and *touched* Jesus' coverings, where, in fact, she was apparently healed.

When people first hear of the story of the woman with the faith healing touch, they *marvel* at her perseverance and belief. But as a survivor of Depression, I was personally moved by something completely different.

What impacted me most about that story was Jesus' *response* to the woman, *after* she touched him directly.

The Bible shares that *when* the afflicted woman touched Jesus' clothes, he felt his *power* leave him; where in response to this withdrawal, he said, "*Who* took my power?" (Mark 5: 21-34).

This might sound like an insignificant remark from Jesus, *until* you examine the dynamics a little closer. The woman, who touched Jesus' clothes that day, did so *without his permission*. In other words, her intent was to *meet her personal needs* without considering how her actions might *impact* Jesus.

However, even Jesus, who was known as a man of Agape love (unconditional love) did *not* allow the "withdrawal" go un-noticed or without accountability. Instead, *when* he had something of his taken *without his consent*, he directly asked and identified, "*Who* took my power?"

MEMO FROM NORMAL LAND®:

"We are to give, what we have to give,
when we have to give it,
and to whom we want to give it to."

Becoming Aware

The story of Jesus and the woman in the crowd impacted me so greatly because Jesus' response to the woman was a fantastic example of something I call Environmental Management.

Environmental Management is the discipline of learning to examine the *situations* we are was exposed to, and then with personal insight, consciously become *aware* as to how these "situations" make us *feel*. Meaning, from what we eat, to what we listened to, to what we wear, to the places we attended, and most importantly, to *whom* we surrounded our self with, we must learn to *listen* to our body and emotions; and *identify* how they make us *feel*. Or more storyline related, we must *monitor* our environments, and directly ask, "Who (or what) is stealing our power?"

MEMO FROM NORMAL LAND®
"Awareness is your first point of healing."

One Step Forward, Three Steps Back

Environmental Management might sound like an easy task to some. But unfortunately for me, it wasn't. Due to the years of abuse, I had become a black belt in emotional numbing; a coping and disassociation technique abuse victims use to survive the pain.

Developing the skill of monitoring my environment required me to become *"present."* Meaning, I had shown up to the here-and-now, which was a tool I simply didn't have.

The end result was a season of emotional tug-of-war where I would take one-step forward and three steps back in my recovery. For example, at times I would step into my "now" with clarity and calm. But before I knew it, "the present" would overwhelm me, and with fear, guilt, anger and powerlessness, I would retreat in my world of disconnect.

Nerice gently reminded me during those painful "present" moments that my job was not to judge or "do" anything about my uncomfortable situations. She would advise me that my job at that point, was only to become *aware* of my emotional environment; and identify *how* it made me *feel.* Nerice repeatedly told me that if I could learn the discipline of staying connected to my "now", and more importantly *own* it *in its entirety,* one day my world of powerlessness and powerful would eventually merge. And guess what? She was right.

It was a few months into my Environmental Management project, when I got invited to a Barry Manilow concert.

I am sure you know Barry Manilow. He is a ballad composer from the 70's who sings about the pathetic side of love; which on a side note, I would *never* recommend while battling depression.

Anyway, it was somewhere between his song "Mandy" and "I Write the Songs" when I thought I was going to either stab my eyeballs out, or take a leap off the balcony. Suddenly in the midst of my painful present moment I had a *conscious* thought shift. It said, "This does not feel good to me. Do something!"

On the surface, this might not sound like a big deal. But it was huge deal for me, as it was the *first* time in a non-crisis situation that I felt complete clarity and control over my emotional status, physical being, and choices. Meaning, rather than retreating inside myself and go numb; continuing to do something that was killing me (emotionally speaking); feel guilty about who paid, how much they paid, or worry about whose feelings I might hurt, I instead owned that *"the situation"* was *not* good for me, and I did something to create immediate change. In other words, I *identified* what was *stealing my power* and then with only a brief apology, I got up and left.

MEMO FROM NORMAL LAND®
"If it doesn't feel good to me, it is not good for me."

Joy Has an Address

My journey out of depression and into Joy took several months of active awareness, and to be honest, it took a few years to finally master it. But over time I developed a four-part Environmental Management system which to this day, navigates me *away* from the environments that cause me depression, and leads me to towards the places that give me Joy. My three-steps to Joy include:

1) Learning to *recognize* my "slip zone" environments.
2) Learning to *identify* the various people, places and things that have the power to steal my joy.
3) Learning to embrace the fact that in living in Joy, (and maintaining a joy-filled environment), is *my* responsibility, and I have the power to choose it for myself.

This very valuable lesson was brought to the foreground of my insight when one day, a man named Dave imparted something to me that I will never forget.

Dave was a gentleman who worked as a front office manager at a small company I frequented. Dave literally marveled me because to this day he was probably one of the happiest men I have ever met. I say that because every time I saw Dave, he was singing or laughing or smiling about *something*. And one day while depression and I were arm wrestling for my soul, I looked at him with vulnerability and asked, "How do you do that, Dave? How do you so easily find your Joy?"

He said words that I will never forget: "Well Tracy, *no one is going to do it for me.*"

MEMO FROM NORMAL LAND®
"My Joy is non-negotiable."

21

Session is In

NERICE: "How are you feeling?"

ME: **"Guilty."**

NERICE: "What do you feel bad about today?"

ME: "Everything..."

NERICE: "So, of all the emotions we have to choose from, you choose guilt?

ME: (Blank stare and long pause) "I didn't know there were other selections on the menu."

Session is Out

Step 4: Breaking Up with Guilt

Journal Entry - July 28 (Year 6)

"If I had a middle name I think it would be 'I'm Sorry.' "'I'm sorry' the sun did not come up on time. 'I'm sorry' you are in a bad mood (and think I'm the cause.) 'I'm sorry' I cost you money or I awoke in your world today. 'I'm sorry' I EXIST."

If someone asked me years ago what I ate for emotional breakfast, which emotional designer I wore, or the name of my stretchy emotional perfume, my answer to all three questions would be, "Oh, that would be GUILT, thank you very much."

Guilt, as a first line response, was the foundation of my character. Doused in it through religion and "parenting skills" as a child; then surrounded with "Professional Guilters" (meaning those who tossed it *on* me like salad dressing), as an adult. The emotion of *guilt* was not only what I felt, it seemed to be who I *was*.

At the height of my emotional shackles, I can honestly say that guilt affected almost every area of my life. For example, I had *unwarranted* guilt from the years (according to Erik) that the sun did not come up on time. I had *shame-based* guilt because I never seemed to be *enough* for Erik (a side effect of living in Narcissistic Abuse). I had *personal* guilt for maybe causing, or *not* stopping the abuse? I had *religious* guilt for getting a divorce. I had *spiritual* guilt for being a "flaw on the church." And I even had something called *"Survivors Guilt,"* which is a form of guilt that describes someone who, once he or she begins to experience the fullness life has to offer, feels as though they are *betraying* those who are still suffering.

And let me tell you, I had a lot of Survivors Guilt: I felt guilty knowing there was a safer place for me *away* from Erik. I felt guilty because I didn't want to go back to a life of pain. I felt guilty about leaving Erik in his misery and ache. And I felt super guilty that I had *no* desire to include him in my future; a future I knew could be amazing, as long as I remained on my path of healing.

Is Guilt Necessary?

On a professional level, I understand why industry and religious leaders say we need a certain amount of *healthy* guilt to maintain a proper moral code or balanced ego. We're *supposed* to feel *moments* of remorse when we step outside our personal integrity arena; or when we've *intentionally* harmed another person.

That however is just the problem. "Moments" of guilt, means that guilt is to have a beginning, middle and end. Which *that* is *not* the type of guilt most trauma abuse victims experience. In abusive relationships, guilt is used as a tool of control on a daily basis. As a result, most survivors are over-saturated in the vice-gripping stuff, so much that one more drop of the emotional poison could easily send us over the edge. *Even* if that drop is delivered as "good" advice, or even if it's considered "God's" advice.

Guilt Serves No Purpose

I understand the concept of guilt-*free* living might go against the moral code of many. I understand it's a difficult prescription to swallow; especially to those who believe that "Godliness", "concerned love" or "good parenting" means serving super-sized portions (of guilt) to those we "love."

I think, however, that's just my point. In case you didn't get the Memo from Normal Land: We are *not* to be the "God" or the "parent" of another adult. Meaning, it's not our job to raise another grown-up, nor (in the case of abuse) are we to be the child of a spouse or a lover.

By the time we are adults, our moral code is to be in place. This means that as free-will beings, we have both the right and the responsibility to make decisions about our life *without* the manipulation, control, *or guilt* of another human being.

MEMO FROM NORMAL LAND®

"People don't want to be controlled.
They want to be loved."

Breaking-Up with Guilt

When I finally made the decision to remove guilt from my emotional system, I must say, it didn't come easy. In fact, when I initially made the choice to release guilt, I had flashes of me sitting in a prison cell with guard rails on my face, and having "Hello Clarise" conversations with my cellmate Hannibal Lector from *Silence of the Lambs*. I honestly feared if I released the emotion of guilt, I might lose my moral compass and swing to the far side of life.

I struggled within myself for quite some time wondering, "If I release guilt, will I lose all care, concern, and compassion? Will I be one of those freaks that run down the street butt-ass naked for no apparent reason? Will I start eating my neighbors for lunch, just like my cell mate Hannibal did? Or will my pendulum swing so far to the left, that I'll lose my conscious for right versus wrong?

I am happy to say that the answer to my fears was "No." When I finally removed guilt's influence from my decision making process, my life didn't fall into demise or into "the hands of the Hell." I didn't start eating my neighbors for lunch (or for dinner, for that matter). Nor did I find my *naked* self in a mug shot on account of a public 100-yard sprint.

When I released guilt from my emotional warehouse, I didn't lose my moral gauge for what was right or wrong. And thankfully, what I eventually discovered was that I could have *never* lost my moral compass for right-versus wrong because to put it bluntly, guilt is *not* a moral, right or wrong issue.

Guilt is nothing more than a true or false emotion. Meaning, it is the *intent* you have behind your decision-making choices. And the *intent* I had behind my difficult choices; choices that included leaving a marriage, filing for divorce, breaking up a "family", not forgiving to the point of forgetting, and refusing to *go along* in the name of "God" any longer, was simply to make life stop hurting.

Meaning, behind my heavily weighted choices that *did* in fact impact others, was simply a *deeply conscious* young woman who was doing the best I knew how, with the limited tools I had, to survive my trauma of abuse.

To make my point clear, I did not need to feel guilt over my choices because my *intent* was *never* to harm anyone. My intent was not to ruin families, or to go against God. My intent was not to destroy finances, homes or images.

Instead, my *intent* as an abuse victim was to make choices so life would *stop* hurting. My intent was to find a safer and kinder place to exist. My intent was to live a life that felt good not just for others, but also that felt good to me; which over time, I learned was one of my birth rights. Meaning, I too had the right to live a life that felt *good* to me. And, during that season of breaking up with guilt, I learned that I had the right to do it, *without* the painful emotion of guilt.

MEMO FROM NORMAL LAND®

"I have the right to enjoy this journey, too."

22

Session is In

NERICE: *"You know you played a role in this."*

ME: (Offended) *"A role?"*

NERICE: *"Yes. You are part of the production."*

ME: *"Well I don't want to be in this production."*

NERICE: *"Then use your legs and walk off the stage."*

Session is Out

Step 6: Breaking Up with Blame

Journal Entry April 13, (year 7)

"I realize that Erik and his family did many horrible things to me. But I must question myself... what was wrong with me that I tolerated this treatment? What's prompted me to go back for more?"

It was about two months shy of our one-year mark, and Nerice and I had made a tremendous amount of progress in my healing: We had worked on *my* learning to accept the truth about what had happened to *me*. We had worked on *my* giving back the wrongly induced pain caused to *me* by others. And we even worked on *my* holding other people accountable for their actions against *me*.

Then, on this particular afternoon, Nerice put a shift in my healing and dropped a bomb on *me*. Our conversation went something like this:

NERICE: "Tracy, you know you played a role in this."

ME (defensive and offended): *"I* played a role in this?! Don't you remember *I* am in counseling because of what Erik and his family did to *me*? *I'm* the one who was victimized by *their* choices. Do you not recall that *I* am the one who has spent the last year rebuilding myself!"

NERICE: "Yes, that is true. Erik and his family did some pretty bad things to you. In fact, they did some very unacceptable things. And I don't take *that* reality or pain away from you, at all.

But Tracy, if you want to reach a place of authentic healing, you *must* eventually stop blaming Erik for the pain and suffering you experienced, and take more ownership of *your* life. Meaning you must embrace the fact that *you* also had your part in the production."

I paused and reflected on her words. Up to that point, I did in fact blame Erik and his family for basically, *everything*. I blamed them for my pain. I blamed them for the craziness. I blamed them for the dysfunction, and the chaos. I blamed them for my lost dreams, my financial ruin, as well as my no-name, stressed induced illnesses. I blamed them for my lack of connection, for losing my job, and I even blamed them for my chronic case of P.M.S.

I'm sure you think I mean P.M.S. where your hormones go nuts, and you feel as though you'll shortly follow. But I don't. I'm talking about a case of P.M.S. that stands for the "Poor Me Syndrome." It's a syndrome I nicknamed that identifies the response of a perpetual abuse victim (speaking of *me* of course), where *after* you have been violated, you can pitifully say, "Poooor Me. They hurt me *again*."

I looked at Nerice in silence. I wanted to challenge her on her "advice." I wanted to tell her she was *wrong* and that I *fully* disagreed. To be honest, I wanted to stop the session and have my own P.M.S. party. But before I could, she leveled me *again* by saying, if I didn't stop blaming Eric and his family for my pain, I would become stuck in my *Self* Induced Misery.

Pardon, but did she say my *Self*-Induced Misery? As in I am doing this to *myself*?

I was shocked. Why in the bloody Hell would I choose to inflict pain on *my* life? I *hated* the hurt I was going through. I detested the trauma wounds. I loathed the lack of power I felt at times. So why would I purposely *choose* to allow this personal destruction to happen to me?

MEMO FROM NORMAL LAND®

"The majority of pain we experience
is pain we induce on our self."

The Payoff

I didn't realize it at the time, but in my relationship with Erik I was getting what is called, a "payoff." I know, *shocking. I was* getting a payoff.

A "payoff" in a relationship is a give-to-get situation where one member of the relationship *gives* a certain something, with the goal of *getting* a certain benefit in return.

As Nerice so clearly pointed out, my payoff in the relationship happened when (in the name of "love and marriage") I voluntarily *gave* my Personal Power to Erik; then, when he destroyed my life, I had the convenience of *blaming* him for *my* lack of happiness - *rather than owning responsibility for it myself.*

"Ouch," was about all I could muster. In reflection, it happened *not* just in my relationship with Erik, but in fact, in *all* of my relationships. My pay-off pattern was one where I would "fall in love" and soon thereafter, hand my Personal Power, my happiness, my health, my safety, and my security, over to the one I "trusted"; *even if that person had not fully earned my trust;* even if they never *asked* for my trust. By habit, or by years of female examples before me, the moment I fell in love I would automatically give control, direction, and the influences of my life to the person in my viewfinder. Then, when they let me down (which was more often than not) I could convincingly *blame* them for my personal pain.

I unhappily discovered that day that Nerice was *correct*. I *was* getting a personal payoff in my relationship. And though I never *caused* the abuse or asked for it, I did, in fact, have a part in the production, every time Erik acted inappropriately, and I *allowed* his abuse by releasing my Personal Power to him.

Personal Power

In many cultures around the world, it's common for women to release their Personal Power in the name of "Love."

Some of us unclutched (our power) because Cinderella-type societies taught us that *someday, our Prince will come*. For others, we forfeited our power because culturally we're taught it's not feminine to have Personal Power.

For me however, the reason I so easily gave-away my Personal Power was because quite honestly, *I didn't know I could have Personal Power*. Meaning, I never got the *Memo from Normal Land* that told me I could be my own North Star, or that I had the right to orbit around my own sun. I never got the guidance that said (*without* suffering from guilt or punishment) *I could be the boss of me*.

In fact, I was destructively taught the *polar* opposite. My life examples showed me that as a female, my "place" was to either, orbit *around the sun* of another person, and if not, be punished for it. Or, to fearfully *serve and sacrifice for "The Son"*. and if not, burn in Hell for it.

Sadly, the life-surviving information that ensured that I would be okay/pure/good/enough/protected and safe if I followed *my* first voice, and trusted *my* personal path, was *never* delivered to my inbox. So in response, I blindly stumbled into my adult life believing that to survive, I had to *serve* others by making *them* my higher power, my North Star, or best said, "The Boss of Me."

The Three Finger-Point Circle of Healing

Several years ago, in my in-depth studies with abuse recovery, I identified three specific phases in the healing cycle of abuse. I call the process The Three -Point Circle of Healing.

Finger-Point Number One: "It's All My Fault"

In the Finger-Point Circle of Healing, phase one is identified as the "It's All My Fault" Phase. I entitled this phase, "It's All My Fault" because this best describes the mindset of an abuse victim; they *authentically* believe, "It's ALL my fault."

The "It's All My Fault" phase is the most *powerless* and painful stage of the cycle, because, during this phase, the big fat finger of blame is pointed directly at the abuse victim. Consequently, the victim then owns this blame and takes the burden and the bullets for *everything* that goes wrong, both in, and outside of the relationship.

The "It's All My Fault" phase is the longest running stage in the cycle of healing, and unfortunately, it will *not* stop or change until the victim of abuse gets help.

Finger-Point Number Two: "Admittance and Accountability"

The second phase of healing I identify as the "Admittance and Accountability" Phase. During this phase of healing, the abuse victim is fueled by newly discovered, self-help wisdom. With that force, she takes a gigantic, courageous step of self-protection and pushes the big accusing finger of blame clockwise (90 degrees *away* from her) and *points it directly at those who wrongfully caused the harm.* And let me tell you, this step feels wonderful.

In the "Admittance and Accountability" phase, the abuse victim starts doing things such as holding their violators *accountable* for their actions. She learns life-skills tools such as boundaries and personal rights. She gets a clear understanding that the violations against her were *wrong.* And she starts sharing *everything* she's discovered about healing to almost *anyone* who will listen.

In phase two, the abuse victim experiences a tremendous amount of healing because it's during this phase that we make three awareness statements about abuse clarity. These life-giving statements are: "This is what happened." "This is who did it." And "It was *wrong!*"

MEMO FROM NORMAL LAND®
"I don't need your stamp of approval on my pain.
If I say it hurts, then it hurts."

Finger-Point Number Three: "Self-Responsibility"

Following the "Admittance and Accountability" phase of healing, there is a third stage of recovery I call the "Self-Responsibility" Phase.

This final phase of healing takes place *after* we have taken the blame off us, and *after* we've held our violators accountable for their actions, *whether they admit it or not.*

In this pivotal, but often *not* achieved phase of healing, we abuse survivors move the finger of blame one more time *off* the violator and (*believe it or not),* clockwise onto us. Only this time rather than the finger being an icon of *blame,* it is instead a loving and non-judgmental signal of *self*-accountability and responsibility.

The "Self-Responsibility" Phase of healing is an exciting step in the cycle because this is where the real traction of self-empowerment begins. In fact, it's during this phase that we find the one thing that has eluded us for years, which is our *Personal Power.*

In phase three of the cycle, we take the reins of control of healing and start including *our self* in the storyline of responsibility. Meaning, we start examining how, why, and where *we* lost the power to navigate our life (in the first place). In phase three we not only start taking ownership of our self *in our present,* but we also begin taking responsibility of what we will *do* with our self, from this point forward.

The "Self-Responsibility" phase of healing is imperative to the overall *success* of permanent wellness, because if we *refuse* to merge into this final phase healing, we will remain *stuck* in the unhealthy cycle of "The Blame Game" for years.

Abandoning Our Healing

I mentioned in the prior segment that phase three of recovery is an all-too-often missed step on the road to healing. I say that because more often than not, many abuse survivors during phase two of the Finger-Point Cycle of Healing, will crawl on the couch of *other* blame, and then slam the brakes of progress on their recovery.

But why wouldn't we? The people who did us wrong are *finally* being held accountable for their idiotic actions! The burden of blame is off our shoulders. We have broken the bondage of silence and are screaming our truth from the top of our lungs. Its visibility and vocality is nothing short of liberating!

To be honest, all this *other* blame feels like we have found our formula for healing. So with our newly empowered soul in place, we settle in on the couch of Phase Two and almost ask as for a cigarette because we think our work is complete.

I must forewarn you, though; this is by no means the finish line of healing. In fact, if we park our self in the *It's All Their Fault* phase of the cycle; or if we "end" our healing by keeping the finger of blame directed at those who caused our injuries, in time we will only reinjure our self.

The best analogy I can use is to compare the couch at Phase Two, to the process of making wine. Like wine, along the journey to healing it *is* important to be in a holding pattern and allow things to ferment for *a while*. But if you stay in that place for too long, you will begin to sour.

MEMO FROM NORMAL LAND®

"There must come a time when it is no longer about them."

Along the journey to healing, there is certainly a season where our storyline needs to focus *only* on our violators. In other words, there is a time and place where, for accountability purposes, they must take the *blame* for *all* that transpired.

Over time however, if we remain playing The Blame Game by pointing the "all responsibility" finger at him (or her or them), it will eventually prohibit us from healing from him (her or them); *because we have not broken away, from "him" (her or them.)* In turn, the on-going dynamic harms us because our *connection* with him (her or them) then keeps us *disconnected* from the important person called Self. Which that then, blocks us from acquiring the *Individuality* and *independence* we *need* to heal, and most important, to reclaim our life and our Personal Power.

Finding Your Personal Power

I don't know about you, but the term *"Personal Power"* eluded me for years. For whatever reason, the pumped-up words always sounded so Super Hero-ish to me. Every time I heard the phrase I envisioned that somehow if I were fortunate enough to become infused with the magic of Personal Power, ginormous letters would suddenly manifest themselves on my bright red T-shirt. Then once on *display, I* could chest-butt anyone who tried to walk on me. "That's right (boink-boink). I've got *Personal Power."*

I know I'm not alone in my Personal Power blur. Many people who feel *powerless* don't understand what this recovery catch phrase means either. Therefore, for that sake of inappropriately chest-butting a stranger, or from wearing a super lame T-shirt, allow me to share what I've discovered Personal Power is, and what it means to me.

What is Personal Power?

My journey to Self-Love has taught me that in general, Personal Power is the ability to make life-giving choices for Self. "Self" being defined as our beliefs, values, preferences, physical body, finances, dreams, desires, and most important our soul, which is our mind, will and emotions.

Specifically, Personal Power is the ability to maintain the influences and authority over the well-being of our life. That means it is the power we possess to *change* our current situation if it shifts into something we don't like, or don't want. And more so, it is the power to *keep* our self on track, *in spite* of what is *on* our track, as we venture through life.

Personal Power is having the strongest *first voice* in our life. It is the wisdom to distill that voice of any emotional toxins that are not yours, or no longer work for you. And it is the confidence to express that voice without the fear of judgment or rejection.

Personal Power is having an up-to-date awareness of Self. Meaning, it is knowing what is right for you, or not; who you are, or who you are *not*. And most important, it is knowing what is yours to own, and what is *not*.

Personal Power is having the ability to have an all-encompassing acceptance of Self, including the compassion to accept where you have been, as well as the awareness of where you are going.

It is the assurance (in Self) to show up in your "Now"; meaning, to take up a certain amount of space in your "today", and to secure that space (with all of your flaws, faults, and *FantasticNess*) without apology.

Personal Power is the ability to have a foundational base grounded in Self-Love. Self-Love, being the conscious relationship you have *with* yourself; being the ability to care for yourself (on a physical, emotional, financial and spiritual level); and it is having the esteem for yourself, which is the ability to make life-giving choices that keep you physically, emotionally and financially, safe.

Finally, Personal Power is the skill of "mid-wifing" yourself to your Authentic Self. Specially this means operating from a standpoint of conscious, self-partnership where you know how to rescue and *reclaim* that Authentic Self if it gets lost. It is having the courage to embrace that Authentic "Self" for who are you are *today*. And most important, it is having the steadfastness to redefine and reinvent that "Self," to its greatest potentiality, when the time is right.

MEMO FROM NORMAL LAND®

"I have a right to be me,

without apology."

23

Session is In

"I want to tell you a story. There was once a woman who wanted all of the wisdom of the world. So she sought out a Monk and asked him to teach her all he knew. The Monk agreed and took her to an empty room at his monastery.

The next morning when the Monk entered the room, the woman rose and warmly greeted him. But without warning he took a 2 x 4 and whacked her across the head. The woman fell to the ground and in pain and confusion. The Monk looked back at her, but she said nothing. So the Monk then left and did not return for another 24 hours.

The next day the Monk returned. Again the woman rose and warmly greeted him. Again the Monk hit her with a 2 x 4. And again she fell to the ground in pain, cried and said nothing. The Monk then left and did not return for another 24 hours.

On the third day the Monk entered the room and was holding the 2 x 4. He raised the wooden paddle but this time the woman stood to her feet, grabbed hold of the Monk's arm and sternly said, "NO MORE!" The Monk then lowered his arm, smiled at the young woman and said, "Now you have learned all the wisdom you need to know in life."

Session is Out

Step 7: Breaking Up with Violators
(Learning Boundaries)

Journal Entry February 28, (Year 7)

"I disconnected my phone today and completely cut-off contact with Erik and his family. Holly called and left me one of the nastiest, hate-filled messages I have ever heard.

To this day, I am still amazed at how they feel they have the right to say whatever they feel and think, to anyone they think deserves it; and to do it without a second thought as to how it might affect that other person's life.

Perhaps this stems from the verbal attacks their delicate lives were punched with as children. Perhaps they are just bad people. Whatever it is, it doesn't matter anymore. I have finally made the decision to no longer be their punching bag.

For a moment today, I almost bought into their crazy lies. But luckily, my healthy internal voice stood strong; and in the midst of the attack, I reminded myself that no matter how much God, my friends, or my family love me, the only person who can control what enters my life is me. The only person who can protect me, and provide safety for me, is me. I have to remember that if I don't protect my heart, my safety, and my emotional well-being, no one else will. I must be responsible for Me."

MEMO FROM NORMAL LAND®

"If someone can't respect the boundaries you've set,
it is your responsibility to make sure they do."

Women in abusive relationships don't understand *a lot* of things, about a lot of things. It's as though we enter this journey without the official *manual* on how to "do" life or love; then consequently, stumble our way from one catastrophe to the next.

There is one thing I can say about this missing manual: As long as we don't have it, life will hurt.

Memos from Normal Land

Along my journey to healing, I did something significant about this missing memo book. I created what I call "Memos from Normal Land."

I came up with that name when one day I was watching a friend of mine "do" life properly. Someone was pushing her limits and without missing a beat, she shut-down the inappropriate behavior and quickly established (to the boundary violator) *where* her personal property lines were staked.

I listened carefully to her selection of words, as well as to the tone of her voice; and I thought to myself, "How did she know how to do that?" I convinced myself there was a secret manual distributed to all the "normal" people that shared the secret rules of love and life.

In case you were curious, that was the birthing place of my Memos from Normal Land®. And from that point forward, my goal was to get that golden list distributed to everyone who needs it.

The Missing Memo called Boundaries

One of the many missing memos we abuse victims never received is the memo about *boundaries*. That, in a nutshell, is why we have *no idea* where our life ends, and where other people's lives begin. Nerice described the condition as "Fuzzy Boundaries"; and it defined me to a tee.

I say that because for the majority of my adult life, *anyone* who wanted to enter my world could walk through my boundary-less doors and say and do whatever he or she wanted. Then to make matters worse, rather than get angry about their violation *and do something to end the pain*, I would instead reward my violator with "good girl" or *polite* behavior, and not let them reap what they had sowed.

What's a Boundary?

A boundary, as defined by Merriem-Webster.com, is a line or border that marks the *limits* of an arena. In other words, it's "the buck stops here" and more important the *"no"*, that establishes (to all concerned) what part of the playground is community property; and what part is off limits.

My Missing Off Limits List

I am sure it can go unsaid, but when I initially entered into recovery, one of the first lessons I had to learn, was the one on boundaries.

I recall in one of my first sessions with Sara, her handing me an extensive, bullet-point, line item list that (according to *boundary regulations)* outlined everything I was responsible for; as well as everything apparently I had to put behind my "personal property line." I remember thinking, "My *what?*"

The list included every part of my physical, emotional and spiritual being, plus my financial status, my thoughts, feelings, choices, beliefs, opinions, behaviors, talents, dreams, values, attitudes, limits, as well as many other things I was still trying to grasp existed.

If that was not enough, I was then told about a *fence.* Specifically, it was an "emotional fence", that *I* was to apparently "build." This particular fence consisted of six "pillars of protection" designed to safeguard my current well-being, as well as provide *protection for the rest of my life.*

And I wonder *why* I was so confused about boundaries? The subject was massive.

Our Issues

Allow me to sidebar for a moment and discuss the topic "issues." I have a quirky belief about the "issues" we face. I believe when we arrive on this journey called life, we have two, maybe three core issues that we are to spend a lifetime unfolding. I believe these issues are our life's work, and part of our happiness comes in identifying our core issues and then discovering the valuable lessons that accompany them.

I also believe that if and when we don't deal with our core issues, our pain will, in a sense "leak", which that energy will start to attract *more* issues, to get our attention. In case you did not know, that's how we become a person with *a lot of issues.*

I believe the process of becoming a person *without* issues reverses itself when we make the conscious decision to heal. When we do, our secondary (or tertiary) layers will shed themselves somewhat easily, which then brings us back to our original core issue (to ultimately learn); which for me was "Boundaries."

"No" is a Love Word

I remember handing the bullet-point boundary list to Nerice, and with complete overwhelm, telling her I had no idea where to begin. She graciously responded by saying, "Let's start at *No.*"

"No?" I asked with confusion.

"Correct." She responded.

"Why 'No'" ? I inquired.

She then said words I will never forget. She said, "Because 'No' is a Love word, Tracy."

My Journey to No

To be honest, when Nerice initially introduced me to the concept of "No", being a love word, I couldn't wrap my brain around the thought. In fact, the idea was so foreign to my base of "normal", I rejected it at first.

"How could 'No' be a love word!?" I challenged. I was taught since childhood that "No" (or what I would later learn was a boundary) was a *bad* thing! My belief system had branded me with layers of anti-no messages ranging from, "You can't say *no* if a young man asks you to dance (or go on a date.)" Or, "If God calls you to Siberia, you can't say *no*!"

From the young age of *I can't remember,* and before I had a fighting chance, religion, culture, and even parenting programmed me to believe that saying "No" was an act of cruelty or rebellion. I was trained to believe that if I said "No," people, parents, and even God would become *angry* with me. And if they became angry, they, in turn, would leave, reject or abandon me; which to the ears of a love-hungry child felt like a kiss of death.

Today, I am happy to share that my long-standing *core* lesson with boundaries has greatly expanded. For example, I have grown to embrace the extensive bullet-point list of responsibilities that are mine to own. I now understand the areas of my "personal being" that I'm required to protect, and *why* it is I need to protect them. Best of all, today (because I got the proper Memos from Normal Land) I now know *how* to build that proverbial "fence of protection" around my mind, body and soul, for the well-being of my life.

It has been a 20-year learning lesson filled with masses of information, personal expansion, and life-skill building. And all of it started by learning the importance and purpose of the small word, "No."

It is recognized as one of the shortest words in the English language, but with this little powerhouse, we are armed with one of the strongest tools we can possess for the protection of our life. With this one-word force, we can establish our visibility to those around us. We can instruct people how to treat us. And we can clearly identify to both others and our self *where* our life begins, and where other people's life ends.

"No" statements such as, "*No*, that doesn't work for me." "*No*, I don't like that." "*No*, that's not my job." "*No*, I won't do that," "*No*, I don't agree." Or my personal favorite, "*No*, I won't give that up for you, or for anyone" are our "No" based *non-negotiables* that lead us to Self-Love.

In fact, "No" is by far one of the *most important* ingredient required for healthy Self-Love (and other love) because "No" gifts us with *limits*. Limits that establish what we will accept, and what we won't; limits that keep the good in, and the bad, out. And limits that allow us to be who we are, and to most important to our healing, to discard who we are *not*.

MEMO FROM NORMAL LAND®

"Love has limits."

24

Session is In

ME: *"I think I am possessed."*

NERICE (calmly): *"Why do you think that, Tracy?"*

ME: *"Because something bad is happening inside of me. One moment I'll be fine. Then in the next, something from the core of my being erupts. It is like an internal violent implosion that shoots through every fiber of my being; and when it does, all I want to do is destroy something or hurt someone."*

NERICE (with a smile): *"Oh Tracy, don't worry. You're not possessed. You're just beginning to get angry!"*

Session is Out

Step 8: Breaking Up with Anger

Journal Entry (Year 7)

"I want to know why! I want to know WHY! I want to know WHY! WHY! WHY! WHY! WHY!!!!"

It was about a year into my healing when I entered into my Anger stage of grieving, and to say the least, I was not happy. In fact, I was bitter, toughened, explosive, and most noticeably pissed-off beyond all rhyme and reason.

In hindsight, I shouldn't have been surprised my anger arrived. For several months "she" clearly let me know she was in route.

I say that because just before *her* arrival my personality started to show a shift. It was like the Dr. Jeckll / Mr. Hyde syndrome where calm, "go along" Tracy was bizarrely being replaced by "explosive time-bomb Tracy"; a person who would cry at one moment, then rage and want to destroy something (or someone) for almost no reason, in the next.

When my Anger initially surfaced, I tried to pretend, or more honestly *deny* that it existed. And I *semi*-accomplished that task by doing what many "anger-denial" types do: I turned my anger inward, into something called *Cold Anger*, which is an inward expression of anger directed against Self.

When Cold Anger manifests itself in our body, we suffer from things like body aches, headaches, insomnia, eating disorders, stomach problems, back issues and many other aches and pains we try to blame on the unknown. There is no question our body reacts to the emotional food we feed it. And for a very long time, I consequently suffered *greatly* from my internal diet of unresolved anger.

I am happy to report that throughout my season of Cold Anger, *luckily* I didn't injure anyone outside of myself. That said I did however, manage to *exhaust* most everyone (within earshot) with tales from my **Pissed-Off About Life** book.

Oh, you know *that* book. It is the emotional storage log where we list, date and inventory *all the personal violations* done to us during our abuse.

For the record, it's normal after any trauma to keep a **Pissed-Off About Life** book. And, it can almost go without saying that (during stages of our recovery), most of us can't help but *generously share* the chapters, verses and story lines with most anyone who will give us a stage.

At least that's what I did. Unfortunately, almost everyone who came within earshot, including friends, family, acquaintances and even strangers at the grocery store or gas station, heard about my woes. Upon eye contact, my internal voice would scream "DAMN IT! Don't you know!! My emotions and needs have been suppressed and ignored, *for years! NOW* it is my time to be heard!"

In hindsight, two thoughts come to mind when I think back on that confusing time: 1) Normal response. 2) Oh, so embarrassing.

Hot Anger

As the months clicked by and my unresolved Cold Anger gained pressure, my internal rage started to boil. "Hot Anger" is what they call it. It's a form of anger that percolates in our emotional blood stream, and if it's not dealt with, it *will* eventually blow and scald anyone close enough to its blast zone.

In a nutshell, that describes what transpired with me. In a short matter of time, things that were once *irrelevant* turned into "irritations." Irritations then progressed into *intolerances*. Then before I could stop it, my intolerance towards people, things and situations turned into full-blown, blood-boiling, outer body *rage*. Rage that started as sarcasm and cutting words. Rage that then turned into screaming and yelling. And rage that one day, I am embarrassed to admit, turned into physical violence.

I suppose for the sake of my personal reputation I could leave that ugly detail out of the book. But for many reasons, I can't.

I can't because *honestly speaking* I wasn't initially embarrassed by my aggression. In fact, in a disgusting way I found my anger, or as I reasoned to myself, "my technique of putting people in their place," rather empowering.

According to my justification, people had walked on me for years, so to finally stomp, back *felt good.* And that's exactly what I did. With my Scarlett O'Hara motto, *"As God as my witness, **no one** will ever hurt me again"* I put my sword in my mouth and my temper on my tongue, and I made *sure* to strike first, *anyone* who represented potential harm.

By all evidence, it appeared that Erik had taught me very well. I say that because *everything* he had done to me; meaning every tactic he used to control and hurt me; every sarcastic word he used to shame me; and every dirty look he used to humiliate me, I in turn learned to *pay it forward* - without a second thought on how it would affect the person on the receiving end. That was until the day I got physical.

I don't remember exactly what sent me over the edge that day. All I recall is that in a split second my years of suppressed rage flipped on me, and I retaliated with violence.

It was the first time I had aggressively *physically* touched another person in rage; and to confess, the *ease* and the justification of excuses I used to cross the line, shocked me.

My encounter with physical abuse happened only once on that day, because immediately following my outrage I had a click moment. Or maybe it was more like a Divine Download moment, where in literally a *slap;* I understood *how* the cycle of abuse reproduces itself. Meaning, in a single stinging moment, I understood *how* a child who is raised in an abusive household (one who says they will *never* cause harm), turns into the adult who ravages pain on a spouse or a child. Or, bringing the topic closer to home, I understood how a person who was once the product of abuse, could transition into being the one *inflicting* the abuse.

I understood the progression of unresolved anger because as I stood there with the emotional blood of my actions on my hands, I had now become the newest face and next generation of *abuse.*

The Voice of Anger

In my course *"Breaking Up with Anger"* I open the class by asking an important question: "Is Anger good or bad?" Inevitably, the response I receive is "It's bad"; which this could not be further from the truth.

Believe it or not, anger *itself* is not "good" or "bad." Anger itself is just an emotion. In other words, it is simply a *feeling* we experience when we are ignited by a violation.

What turns anger into either a "good" or "bad" experience is *how* the anger presents itself. Let me explain.

The *emotion* of anger is one of our soul's voices. In other words, it's a messenger anchored deep *within* our emotional system whose primary purpose is to tell us if something is *wrong*.

I like to compare the voice of anger to that of a shoulder-perched angel, who similar to a live broadcaster, communicates its observations about our life directly into our emotional ear. But rather than our messenger being dressed in angelic white and whispering sweet inspirations, she is instead draped in fiery red, screaming at the top of her lungs that she is pissed-off and angry *because we are not listening to her warning signs that she's screaming for the protection of our life.*

MEMO FROM NORMAL LAND®

"Anger is a sign that something is wrong."

The Purpose of Anger

The sole purpose of Anger is to warn us that **something is wrong**. In other words, its job per say, is to speak to us *from within*, and bring to our attention the parts of "us" being hurt, violated, jeopardized or compromised.

When anger sounds its internal voice, its intent is to keep us pro-actively safe. For example, if something "wrong" happens in our *present,* anger will flare its head and warn us that we are in harm's way.

If and when however, we ignored the warning signs of anger and allow the "wrong-doing" to pass without *recognition, restitution* or *resolve*, anger will then become a rooted emotion; one that will continue to sound *until* we directly deal with what *"is"* wrong, or what *"was"* wrong in the past. That is the reason *why* the path to healing from raging anger requires us to give our anger a voice, and ask it the all-important question of "What is wrong?"

What is wrong?

When I *finally* gained the courage to ask my Anger, "What is wrong," it responded by passionately navigating me to the backlog of *unresolved* aches and memories in my soul. Aches and memories interestingly enough, that I *had* cried over countless times (on account of the *wounds* they caused), but I had never *grieved* over the *permanency* of their loss.

It was by no means an easy journey. But one-by-one, as I went to that scary place, I finally gave my anger a voice. And one-by-one I embraced my pain. One-by-one I asked my anger "What is wrong?" And then, for the first time, one-by-one in a healthy way, I allowed myself to grieve my losses, *and get very, very angry.*

My conscious grieving lasted almost six months, and during that time you could say in general, I grieved and got angry over *all* the things that "would of, could of, and should have been." But more specific, I grieved in *detail*, over *every* violation that happened against my body, soul and mind during the years of abuse.

For example, I grieved and got angry over *every* cruel and humiliating word that was ever said to me, as well as every controlling and violating act that was done *to* me. During that season I grieved over the many things that robbed me of my dignity; over the things that suppressed me of my right to Be; and I grieved over the things that denied me of my rights as a human being. The, yes, rightfully so, I got very, very angry.

During that season I grieved over all the physical *things* I lost. Simple things like my high school yearbooks and my furniture, all the way to my house, my car, my credit, my marriage, and the jewelry given to me from my mother. I grieved over being stripped of the *things* that were physically and rightfully mine; and the loss of these *physical* things, (as shallow as it might sound) made me very, very angry.

During that season I grieved over the emotional limbs and the chunks of my life I lost in the name of "love." Meaning, I grieved over the sacrifices of my give-to-get effort that sadly *never* came with a return or repayment. I grieved for that *wrongly* forfeited parts of being, and when I embraced the losses of *me*, I got very, very angry.

During that season I grieved over the post-divorce wreckage. I grieved over the fact that I was struggling hand-to-mouth to relaunch myself, my career, and my economics (that were annihilated in the divorce); all while Erik landed on his feet with a new life, a new house, a six-figure promotion, in a new state, and a clean slate. The injustice of the entire legal process was so very wrong, and it made me very, very angry.

Finally, after several months of processing through all my post abuse emotional wreckage, I arrived at the doorsteps of my last grievance of betrayal (and rage), which I must confess was difficult to embrace. As wrong, as "sinful", as downright abominable as it might sound, my truth was that I was very, very angry, *at God.*

Yes, God. The Supreme Being who as a child I lived for; who as a young adult I was willing to "long suffer" for; and yet who as a victim of repeated abuse, He never showed up to protect. I based my entire belief system and life choices on a Deity that claimed to "love" me, yet who in reality completely failed me. And out of all the tears of anger I cried, it was this out-of-balance relationship, and my commitment to do what is "right" that enraged me the most.

My Friend Called, Anger

My Anger Stage of Grieving was a tear-filled, soul purging season of Awareness. There were times when in the midst of my rage I thought my tears would never end. There was a season where the end seemed nowhere near in sight. And yet, one day it *did* finally lift, I was left with three significant insights and gratitude (believe it or not) about the emotion of anger that to this day I still embrace.

The first thing my season of grieving taught me is that *embracing* anger and walking *through* anger is a necessary step in the healing process. In fact, I learned that until we *get* angry and feel our rage, authentic healing will remain at bay.

Second, I discovered in that when it comes to the undeniable emotion of anger, *getting* angry is much better than *being* angry. In fact, I learned that the *art* of getting angry (which is being able to get angry and not hurt yourself or others) is the only guarantee that Hot Anger won't leave its fingerprints on you, *or on others.*

Third and best of all, during that season of grief I discovered that the emotion of anger *is my friend.* In fact, it's our hard wired *gift* from the Universe; our God-given blow horn per se, that *when* it screams, it's simply doing its job. Which at the end of the day, I've come to believe *is* an act of Love. Love *from* the Universe, who I later realized *did* show-up for me, loud and clear. I just never got the Memo from Normal Land that this Voice of Protection was found *in* my anger; anger that was instilled *in* me to keep me *safe,* and to keep me protected from harm.

25

Session is In

ME: *"No way."* I said emphatically.

NERICE: *"Why not?"*

ME: *"Because after everything I've been through, and after all I've lost, I have absolutely no interest in offering forgiveness to anyone involved in my destruction. In fact, hear me clearly: Not just "No". But absolutely, NO WAY!"*

Session is Out

Step 9: Breaking Up with Un-Forgiveness

It was about a year and a half into my healing when the topic of Forgiveness came onto the table. Quite honestly when Nerice first mentioned it, the thought both repulsed and violated me.

To my ears of recovery, "forgiveness" sounded more like the modern day "F" word, than the next step to healing and empowerment.

My History with Forgiveness

I don't know your reference point with forgiveness, but candidly speaking it had *never* been a feel-good topic for me. From the time I was a child, pulpit preachers infused me with the belief that it was my *obligation* "to forgive *anyone* who committed a wrong *against* me."

In fact, they told me if I didn't forgive those who "sinned" against me, then "God would *not* forgive me for my sins." So, out of sheer fear and survivorship (at an age too young to make life commitments) I adopted a "*must* forgive" mentality. Then, in the name of *not* disappointing God, or burning in Hell, I consequently tolerated boundary violators for years.

And So It Transferred

Erik, without a doubt, was one of the many boundary violators who took advantage of my *all-forgiving* nature. Sadly, he viewed my religious obligation *to* forgive, as his personal trump card to violate.   For example, if Erik cheated I was expected to forgive. If he abused, I was expected to forgive. If he spent money we didn't have, I was expected to forgive.

According to Erik, forgiveness was his "right to violate." So when Nerice suggested I consider *forgiving* Erik for his violations against me, my response was easy. I reflected on my history and without a second thought, looked Nerice in the eyes and emphatically said, "Forgive HIM?! No way!"

Help, My Walls are Cracking

It was initially easy for me to *not* extend an olive branch of forgiveness to Erik. That's because I had spent the entire prior year building a wall of "un-forgiveness" around myself.

You could say that my wall of un-forgiveness was a form of protection per say; an insurance policy of sorts, to make sure I *never* went back to Erik again. So to guarantee my success, I consciously and carefully built an emotional wall around my heart, and used every prior violation as a brick in its foundation, and sealed the wall in place with oil deep levels of hate.

For over a year, my wall of "un-forgiveness" (oozing in its constant reminders of past violations) kept me just angry *enough* at Erik, to keep him away. Then, suddenly something started to shift: My once *healthy* anger started to turn into sour *bitterness*. My "accountability sharing" merged into repeat stories of victimization. And most evident, my internal *hate* towards Erik, (hate that initially fueled my anger and healing) started to feel more like a physical weight and burden, rather than an internal shield of safety.

The Secrets of the Heart

A few days after my session with Nerice I was flying to Sacramento, California for work. On that particular morning, I was *not* in a good emotional space because for days I had been festering over an old "Erik wound."

I was revisiting the violation in my mind's eye when subconsciously I began doodling in my journal. For about twenty minutes I mulled over the miserable memory, and when I looked down at the paper in front of me, *I had subconsciously drawn a heart that I darkened with 98% black ink.*

I remember looking at that heart and feeling both sadness and yet intrigue as I *knew* my subconscious blackened doodle was an *exact* reflection of my own heart.

So with my curiosity sparked, I drew another heart and then summoned another bad memory from my vast collection of wounds; only this time, I *consciously* allowed my soul to *feel* the burden of the violation, *while* I doodled.

Again, when finished re-living this miserable memory, my heart doodle was almost fully darkened.

I continued my blackened heart exercise throughout the flight and by the time I landed, I had a Devine Download. My download revealed that for over a year, as a part of my healing, I had *consciously* built a wall of "un-forgiveness" toward Erik.

Initially, that wall was built to keep Erik *out,* so I could feel better. But, as I doodled blacked hearts that day, it was clear that what I had originally created to *protect* my heart, mind, and soul, was now *burdening* my heart, mind, and soul. What I had originally constructed to keep me externally safe, was slowly turning into a form of emotional bondage that was causing me to sink.

As I looked at my blacked hearts, it was suddenly clear that by staying behind this wall of *un-forgiveness,* I was subjecting myself to *reliving* Erik's violations, *a lot.* In turn, it kept me reliving my pain of abuse, *a lot.* And which ultimately kept me reconnected to the original hurt, *a lot.*

MEMO FROM NORMAL LAND®

"Forgiveness is a gift to me."

Like a glass can only hold so much water, I have come to believe that our heart or better said, our soul can also only hold so much emotion.

I mention that because during the post-violation season, it's natural for us to build a wall of "un-forgiveness" around our heart; especially towards those who have the power to *hurt* us again.

Often times, to *not* repeat our past mistakes, we make the conscious effort of building this wall of "un-forgiveness" as a wall of *remembrance.* We then naturally believe that as long as our wall remains erect (and those memories remain on display) our "un-forgiveness" (in a sense) guarantees our healing.

For a season, this wall of "un-forgiveness" *will* most definitely keep us safe. Our hate and anger will ultimately serve as a fuel source that will keep us on track. However, if we keep those trauma memories "fresh"; meaning if we keep our wounds and resentments in our *current* and conscious thought process, our soul will ultimately become burdened by their emotional weight. Then before we know it, the once *protective* wall that we built to keep us protected, will flip on us. And rather than our "un-forgiveness" *serving* our heart, mind and soul with healing, the burden (of the memories) will begin to *rob* us of the happiness and love we need *to heal.*

The Wrong Type of Forgiveness

I will never forget the phone call I received that summer afternoon. It was the well-meaning pastor of Erik's who, after brief introductions said, *"Forgiveness is a **gift** Tracy. It's an Act of Mercy wherein the name of God, we are to **release** the person who violated us, from the responsibility of their sin. (Long pause). Therefore, Tracy, it's time to forgive Erik."*

My response to the unsolicited advice was along the lines of, "Wait. *What"?!*

Why should I, the abuse victim, have to *gift* my violator anything? Wasn't I the one who had precious things ripped and destroyed from my life without permission? Wasn't *I* the one still piecing myself together? Yet *I* am required to *release* the guilty party of the burden and accountability of *their* actions?

The very concept goes directly against the end-goal of healing. Abuse recovery is about *regaining* our personal power over something that *took* our personal power, without consent. It's about us reclaiming our mind, soul, and body, *under our terms.* And it's about doing it on our timing.

On the journey to healing, our motto is not "you are ready for my forgiveness so now you can have it." No. Our motto of empowerment *must* be, that we give what we have to give, when we want to give it, and most important *to whom we want to give it to;* especially when it comes to forgiveness.

<u>MEMO FROM NORMAL LAND®:</u>

**"I give what I have to give, when I have to give it
and to whom I want to give it to."**

A New Definition of Forgiveness

I want to sidebar and share a short story with you. When I was in college, I severely injured my lower back. I was at an event in Ensenada, Mexico, shaving my legs in the shower when the next thing I knew I was on the blue tile floor, naked, gasping in pain, and unable to walk because my back was in complete spasm.

Two days later when I finally got clearance to travel, I returned to the United States and immediately started physical therapy. The only problem was that, this particular doctor did not accept insurance and after several months of treatment I was left with a $3,000 bill; which was a ton of money for a poor college student.

Every month when my invoice arrived, I diligently paid my $100 to the doctor. Then oddly, at seven months, it all stopped.

I phoned the office manager to inquire about my invoice, where surprisingly she told me that according to the records my balance was zero. I assured her there was a mistake because according to my records I still *owed* at least $2,100. But she confirmed, "No Tracy. Your balance is zero. The doctor has *forgiven* your debt."

I share that story because when we come out of abuse, it's normal for us to feel "owed" . Financially, physically, spiritually and for sure emotionally, our pockets have been so deeply dug into that we're not sure *how* healing can be repaid; if *ever* repaid.

As we logically scramble for justice, we reason that, the person who *broke* us, should be the responsible party for fixing us. So in "reason" we look to our abuser to make proper mends for the destruction they caused, but *Memo from Normal Land:* People who break things are *breakers*. It's not within their power to fix it.

That leaves us then with a necessary question required for repair, which is, "Where then, are we to find our repayment for our pain?

The Act of Gifting and Releasing

After much soul searching, I must confess that surprisingly, my journey to healing has led me to *agree* (in part) with the well-meaning pastor. *"Forgiveness is a **gift**, where we are to **release** the person who violated us, from the responsibility of their sin."*

From where I stand today, I fully agree that forgiveness *is* the act of **gifting** and **releasing**. However, rather than the gift and release be given to the person who *caused* the harm, I believe the real beneficiary needs to be the person *inflicted* with the harm. In our case, that means the beneficiary of forgiveness needs to be *you*, where in the name of gifting, *you **release*** your abuser from your heart or head-space; and with it, the harm and the memories they created.

In other words, this means that *you* make the life-giving, conscious choice to remove (or release) the person who injured you from *your* emotional system; so that *you* can be free from *their* "sins", in order for you to heal.

For clarity, releasing your perpetrator doesn't mean *taking* them back, or *going back* to a place of pain. It also doesn't mean *condoning* their actions, or saying it was all "okay." For the record, what they did *is* not "okay"; it *was* not "okay" and it will *never* be "okay." And forgiveness is not about it being "okay."

Forgiveness also has nothing to do with "forgetting" what happened. Because chances are, you might not *ever* forget what happened. But then again, I am not sure we are supposed to.

What Forgiveness Is

If forgiveness is not about releasing the other person, or pretending that in the name of God, it is somehow okay, then what is forgiveness?

To me, forgiveness is the emotional shifting of Energy, where you release (from your emotional system) the negative memories caused by the violator, and exchanging them for a clean and open emotional slate. It's a gift you give *yourself* where, when the time is right, you make the *conscious* choice to set yourself free from the wrongful acts of crime against you.

To me, forgiveness is an act of total selfishness; where in the name of *self*-love (which is the positive relationship you choose to have with yourself), you *consciously* choose to set yourself free from the bad memories of the past. Its where, in the name of *self*-care (which is the intentional act of caring for one self), you choose to move from the slamming emotion of judgment, to the lighter and kinder emotion of acceptance. Which acceptance for the record, *doesn't* mean feelings of "gratitude" or "joy." Acceptance means reaching a point of healing where you can *accept* things for what happened yesterday, and for what they are, today.

Finally, forgiveness is an act of *self*-esteem (which is the confidence you have in your decision-making skills) where when the time if right (and only you know when that is) you release the grip the past had on you, so you can be free to step into your future. A future may I add, that is totally capable of *repaying* you for all you've lost, because *IT* understands all that you survived, to get where you are today.

MEMO FROM NORMAL LAND®:

"Forgiveness is about Me."

26

Session is In

ME *"Nerice, when will all this end?"*

NERICE: *"When you **choose** it.."*

Session is Out

Step 10: Breaking Up with Stuck
(Dreaming, Loving and Living Again)

Journal Entry - September 1 (Year 7)

"It's not necessarily the difficulties that stress me. It's the pressure of making the right or wrong choice that unnerves me the most."

It was two years into my healing when *finally*, the pains of abuse started to subside. As Nerice put it, "The crises seemed to be over."

You would think I would have fallen off my stilettos about that news. But I didn't. Up to that point, my healing and recovery had become my *"everything."* And when I say my everything, I mean my *every-thing*. I had put all my energy and focus on making my present life safe, that I hadn't given much thought (if any) to my *future*.

So there I was: Life-graduation certificate in hand, ready *and able* to move forward into my bright and shining future, but *stuck* in complete fear and paralysis at the doorsteps of my present.

The Fear of the Future

Standing in fear at the doorsteps (of our life) is a common aftermath affect in abuse victims. *Survivorship Syndrome* is what I call it. It's where we get *through* the crisis and heal most of our wounds, but where we never really gain the courage to jump *into* life again.

For the record, we abuse victims don't *intentionally* get stuck at this point of our healing. At our core, we want nothing more than to get on with life and rebuild our ruins. After all, we are completely aware of the time we've lost due to the nonsense of abuse. And we want nothing more than to move beyond it.

However, even if we try, sometimes *we can't*. We can't because without our knowing it, one more layer of post trauma abuse has anchored us by the feet. It is called *Survivorship Syndrome,* and if we are not careful, the stakes it spears can keep us stuck at the door steps of life, for years.

Survivorship Syndrome

The condition of Survivorship Syndrome is a real condition most abuse survivors face. It's a sneaky condition that creeps into our behavior and attitudes, and manifests itself in little ways that most of us overlook. For example, Survivorship Syndrome leaks itself into our thought process and harasses us with *excuses; specifically,* confidence-shattering excuses that chant, "It's too late, too much time has passed", "...there's too much to catch-up on", or "I might not really deserve it" excuses.

Survivorship Syndrome also debilitates us is into *exhaustion.* In case I haven't mentioned, we are *tired*! But then again, of course we are. Healing has taken *every* bit of our energy; yet *now* we're to muster more strength to move on with our life! Its logic seems almost unjust.

The most prominent area Survivorship Syndrome creeps into our life however, is with *fear.*

That's right, *fear;* emotionally paralyzing, life-halting fear. Only, rather than our *fearing* a memory or ghost from our haunting past, we instead are plagued in *complete* fear, of what is unknowingly waiting for us in our *future*.

Living with our Mistakes

At the water cooler station of abuse recovery, there's a common emotion, abuse victims collectively share; that emotion is "O*verwhelmed.*"

Meaning, after everything we've survived, we can't help but look at our situation and feel complete *overwhelm: Overwhelmed* by the time we've lost; *overwhelmed* by the catch-up we have; *overwhelmed* by the mistakes we've made; *overwhelmed* by our list of failures; and worse, *overwhelmed* by the personal pressure we have (on our self) to do things *"right"* this time.

According to our logic, we *have* to get things right this time. The official Master Mistake Checklist shows that we've fulfilled our quota of life failures and mistakes. As a result, we *can't (as in no way in Hell)* put ourselves in the position to try and fail, *again*. Our newly rebuilt self-esteem cannot handle it, *yet*. Our ego (that's taken its public punches) won't handle it, *ever*.

So, rather *than* handle it and move on with our life, we instead buy into the fear, justify that "stagnant" is the better of two evils, and plant our feet at the doorsteps, only to get stuck there for years to come.

It is called Survivorship Syndrome; and if we are not careful, it can be the next excuse to abandon our life.

MEMO FROM NORMAL LAND®

"A mistake is the opportunity to do it better."

It's All Par for the Course

In a moment of compassion, I must say that it wouldn't be normal for us to go through what we have survived and *not* be affected, in some way or another. In fact, we wouldn't be human if we weren't.

Abuse Trauma is devastating. It cuts us to the quick of our being, and I believe it changes us at an emotional DNA level. In defense, we will probably never be the same person we were prior to the abuse. But in all fairness, how can we?

We learned some pretty ugly lessons during our war of survivorship. For example, we learned how to fear another human being; how *not* to trust our self; and question *why* God abandoned us in spite of our effort to do "His Will." We learned to lie for survival; to deny that we were in pain; and as we very well know, we witnessed just how far we would go to survive the insanity.

In hindsight, our season of abuse will never go down in our personal history books as a bright and shining moment. Unfortunately, we will never look at our years of hard work and be proud of getting straight "A's" in mistreatment. To make matters more humiliating, no one is also going to give us a medal of recognition for the pain we suffered either. In fact, most people will continue to silently wonder why we stayed so long; and after a while, so will we.

Choices

I began this book by sharing that my goal in *The Courage to Say "No More"* was to empower the victim of abuse, to repair their life in the aftermaths of trauma. Within that spirit, as we step into the last chapter of my story, there's one final take-away I want you to embrace.

It's a piece of advice centered on a *choice* you will be forced to make when standing at the doorsteps of your future. It's a *pivotal* piece of advice that depending on what you *choose* will either make you a "survivor" of abuse (meaning someone who stands at the doorsteps of your life and stays there). Or, it will make you an "overcomer" of abuse (meaning someone who has the courage to step into their life and reclaim what is *rightfully* theirs).

This important piece of advice centers on the *angle* you will choose to perceive what you've experienced as an abuse survivor. In other words, it's who you will choose to become, and *what* you will choose to become *in spite* of what you have survived.

MEMO FROM NORMAL LAND®

"It is not what happens to you that matters.
It is how you choose to handle what happens to you that counts."

Survivor or Overcomer

I want to share a story with you. When I was first married to my husband, Spyro, we went to Hawaii for a summer vacation. On the third day of our vacation, we were in the water enjoying the

240

day when we started playing a game that we called, "If you do, I DO!" It was a silly Lover's game inspired by the movie *The Titanic*.

The game rules were that if one of us did something brave or unique, the other would proclaim their love and loyalty by saying, "If you do, I DO!" Then as an act of "love", the chanter would proceed to join the other person in the same act of bravery; or whatever.

On that particular day, Spyro was about 10 feet deeper in the waters than I. It was high tide, and the larger than normal waves were breaking on the shoreline behind us.

Spyro was buoying in the deeper waters when suddenly a swell came towards him. To protect himself, he yelled from the distance, "I'm going under!" in which he took a deep breath and disappeared into the ocean.

I watched my darling husband from afar, and in a less-than-brilliant moment, I then said the stupid words, "If you do, I DO!!"

I, however, didn't consider the velocity and speed the wave had gained from Spyro's location to mine, and before I could take a deep breath and head under, I got hit in the face with what felt like a brick wall of water. I was snapped backward, pushed uncontrollably under the strong current and then finally slammed onto the sandy shoreline. It was truly one of my most frightening moments in my adult life.

I desperately crawled my way to the dry sand (bathing suit top no longer in tack), and I heard people screaming. Then, as I spat the water out of my mouth and tried to see through my wet, sandy hair, and burning salt water-filled eyes, I started to cry.

My accident left me traumatized for days. It *also* squelched any desire I had to get into the beautiful blue ocean.

Over the days that followed, Spyro urgently encouraged me to get back in the water and face my fear. His said, if I didn't face it, *then and there*, I might not ever. But I didn't care. After what I experienced, I was *afraid* of the water, and had no desire to go back in again.

I spent the remaining days of our vacation watching Spyro from the shoreline. And though I longed to be with him and share the experience of Hawaii, my fear got the best of me and I couldn't move from my beachside seat. That was until the last day of our trip when just before sunset I got one of my Divine Download moments.

I was standing on the beach watching my husband create good memories for himself, when suddenly my soul said, "This is JUST *surviving* Tracy; where you make it through the trial, but you never attempt to jump back into life again."

MEMO FROM NORMAL LAND®

"We live in choices."

An End in Sight

There Is no doubt that healing from abuse is the fight of your life. There is no doubt that it is a fight that when we're in it, we think it might not ever *end*. It's a fight that when we first heal, it's hard to see an *end* in sight. But, it is *also* a fight that when we do heal, the rawness of what we've experienced *will* eventually start to dissipate. Meaning, along the journey to healing we *will* eventually reach a point where the hard core steps of recovery will be behind us and life will begin to take on *new* paths and *new* journeys of discoveries.

The question then becomes, "When you are at this stage of healing, "*What path will you choose?*" In other words, when you reach that shoreline of life and you realize you *survived* the awful world of abuse, will you finish your recovery journey by crossing the finish line of healing and step into your future? Or will you remain at your doorsteps (or the seashore of life) and *abandon* all you have *yet* to become, in the name of fear?

And here is a word of truth: The path you choose to finish your journey (and yes, it is a choice) will not only affect the quality of your life today, but more so, it will also affect the quality of your life for years to come.

What will you Choose?

It may sound odd that abuse recovery has finish line results. But in all truth, it does. When it comes to healing from the pains of abuse, there *are* two different finish lines we can cross.

A Non-Finish Recovery: In the world of abuse recovery there is something I call a Non-Finish Recovery. A *non*-finish recovery is when we *choose* to remain at the doorsteps of our future by *not* reinventing our life, in the wake of the abuse. A Non-Finish Recovery is when we make the choice to stay paralyzed by the fear of failure, and re-make our self into only a *partial* version of our full potentiality. Or to put it bluntly, it's *choosing* to build a *half-life* in honor of the abuse we survived, by allowing the abuse to define us *long after we survived it.*

A Winning Finish: There is however another finish we can choose for our journey. I call it The Winning Finish of Abuse.

The Winning Finish of abuse happens when *in* spite of what we have survived, we *choose* to become all that we were originally and organically designed to be, *before the abuse affected us.* A Winning Finish in Recovery means that *in spite* of how long it takes to reach the finish line of personal repair, we make the *conscious choice* to shed the definitions abuse tried to put on us, and reinvent our self into the full potentiality of who we have *yet* to become.

MEMO FROM NORMAL LAND®

"We don't have to build an unfinished life
in honor of the abuse we survived."

It's Time to Reclaim Your Life

There is no doubt that abuse is criminal. It's a thief that kills, steals and destroys us at a soul and cellular level. It's a condition that robs us of our love. It takes away our personal possessions. It destroys our dreams. It makes us mistrust other humans. And if lived long enough, it distorts our personal interpretation of *Self*; even sometimes to the point where we question our will to live.

Abuse *is* nasty; so much so, that in the depth of our anger we probably wouldn't wish it on our worst enemy.

But that said, if we're *ever* going to fully heal from what we have survived, meaning if we are *ever* going to rise from its ashes and reinvent our self into something new, there comes a time when we *must* make the conscious choice to "break-up" with the cycle of abuse, and step into our future. That means, there comes a time when we must stop *allowing* the abuse to define us solely on *what happened* to us in the past and instead, learn to define our self on the *overall potential* of who we have *yet* to become.

That means that when we find our self at the doorsteps of our life, at the fork in the road that will determine if we will be a *survivor,* or an overcomer of abuse, there comes a time when we must consciously choose the path of *overcoming.* Meaning, we must look our fear in the face; we must grab our destiny by the bootstraps; then, *without apology,* we must choose to step into a life and future that is rightfully ours.

MEMO FROM NORMAL LAND®

"The greatest revenge to abuse is to live life abundantly."

Taking Revenge on Abuse

In the world of morality, people are often advised to *avoid* revenge. I however disagree; in part, that is. According to *my* world of recovery, I believe revenge is something we *need* in order to bring things into balance. "Justice" is a mandatory ingredient in rebuilding our life on solid ground.

That however, stands on the belief that *revenge* has nothing to do with harming those who caused harm to us. Meaning, revenge in our case, doesn't mean seeking ill-will against the person or people who abused us (as they were only victims of abuse themselves). Instead taking "revenge" against abuse means to take *satisfaction,* or in other words to find *pleasure* in *restoring* our life, to everything it can be, in spite of the abuse.

Specifically, "revenge" against abuse means *reclaiming* and reinventing our self into *everything* the abuse said we *would* never be; *could* never be; or ever *deserved* to be; *in spite of what was done to us.*

Taking revenge on abuse means reclaiming *all the territories* we surrendered during the years of destruction. It means taking back our dignity, our hopes, our finances, our belief in love, our trust in mankind, our faith in God, our fragile families, our shattered homes, our possessions, our first voice, our self-esteem, or *whatever* is on that long list of destruction we lost; while fearfully enduring the abuse we survived.

Taking "revenge" on abuse means having the *right* to reclaim *our life;* but not just our material possessions and our body. We have the right and responsibility to reclaim our dreams and desires, and our hopes, passions and inspirations as well. In fact, to properly rebuild, we *must* reclaim these life source entities, because they were micro-chipped into our soul at birth, to navigate us to who we are and what we are to become. They *are our internal signposts that lead us back to Self.* And the best *revenge* we can have against abuse is to reclaim these precious life sources; to give them breath and life; and to wave their banner of success in the face of our personal destruction and say, "*In spite* of it all, I still had the power and passion to show up for my life."

Most important though, taking "revenge" on abuse means having the *right* to reclaim our belief in Love again. And by Love, I mean Self-Love, Love for others, and the Universe's Love.

From the first steps of my personal recovery I made a commitment to my journey that said, "Love *must* be the goal of healing." I made that commitment because Love, in its authentic form, is the *polar opposite* of abuse. I made that commitment because "Love" is the most *evidentiary* form of healing we can possess. And most importantly, I made that commitment because as I understood the difference between abuse and love, it was clear to see that where Love is, abuse *cannot be.*

I want you to think about that for a moment, because it is so empowering: Imagine, if we can reach the point where we are *so* grounded in our healing that we have the faith and courage to *believe* in the one thing that nearly destroyed us; then that my friend, *is* the sign of *authentic healing.* It is the banner of genuine restoration. It is the evidence that the past is truly behind us and that the medicine for the broken heart has worked. It is the proof that good people still prevail, and the manifestation that the human soul *can* be repaired. Most enduring however, believing in the beauty of love; meaning, having faith once again in the thing that almost killed us, is a love note (in human form) from the Universe, who is repaying us for all the pain we have endured.

MEMO FROM NORMAL LAND®

"Love is the Goal."

Part V

Recognizing the Signs of Abuse

27

The Abuse Test

The United States Department of Justice defines Domestic Violence (also known as Intimate Partner Abuse) as *"A learned pattern of behaviors used by one person in the relationship, to gain and maintain control over the other person.*

Domestic Violence has no prejudices. It can affect and infiltrate any person or relationship at any stage of life; including if you are married/separated/dating, gay/straight, religious/atheist, educated/uneducated, rich/poor, young/old, black/white, or male and female.

Statistics show that according to the United Nations, one in three women experience physical abuse, internationally. According to F.B.I. reports within the United States, Domestic Abuse affects one in four women. The statistics for men in the U.S.A. are one in eleven.

At the writing of this book statistics remain vague with the number of victims affected by emotional abuse. However, being that one hundred percent of all physical abuse begins with emotional abuse, it can be speculated to be at pandemic levels.

The Abuse Test

To determine if you are suffering from an emotionally abusive relationship, please take the following test. If you check more than three questions, you are in an abusive relationship:

[] Is there someone in your life who is irritated or angry with you several times a week (or more) although you do not mean to upset him or her? Are you surprised each time they get angry? Do they say they are not mad when you ask what they are upset about? Or do they tell you in some way, it's your fault?

[] Do you find when you try to discuss your upset feelings or issue with them they a) refuse to discuss the situation. b) claim you are trying to start an argument? Or c) Are the issues being left unresolved?

[] Do you frequently feel perplexed and frustrated because your lover/partner/mate is unable to understand your intentions?

[] Do you find yourself not necessarily upset about the concrete issues (meaning how much time you spend with each other, or where to go on vacation, etc.) but more so about the communication within the relationship?

[] Do you sometimes wonder, "What's wrong with me? I shouldn't feel so bad?"

[] Do you find that your abuser rarely, if ever, wants to share his thoughts or plans with you?

[] Do you find that your abuser takes the opposite view from you on almost everything?

[] Are you not allowed to say "stop it" without a punishment?

[] Does your lover/partner/mate get either angry, or has "no idea what you are talking about" when you try to discuss an issue with him?

[] Do you feel like a child in the relationship, having to ask permission and apologizing for your behavior? Do you feel powerless and "less than" your lover?

[] Have you stopped seeing your friends and family? Does your lover/partner / mate criticize your friends and family members? Did he/she complain so much in the past that you stopped seeing your family and friends to avoid an argument? Are you ashamed to see your friends or family because of your mate's behavior? Are you embarrassed at having tolerated with so much?

[] Do you believe that you are to blame for your lover/partner/mate's problems? Do you feel you are mostly responsible for the problems with the relationship?

[] Does your lover/partner/mate try to take advantage of you sexually or make unreasonable sexual demands on you, including unwanted sex or the withdrawal of sex?

[] Does your lover/partner/mate's personality change when he drinks alcohol?

[] Does your lover/partner/mate use "humor" to put you down or degrade you?

[] Does your lover/partner/mate lack the ability to laugh at him or herself?

[] Does your lover/partner/mate find it hard to apologize or admit they are wrong? Do they make excuses for their behavior or always blame others for their actions?

[] Does your lover/partner/mate usually get their way in deciding when and where the two of you will go?

[] Does your lover/partner/mate control or disapprove of your spending but has no problems spending on him or herself?

28

The Facts about Abuse

The world of abuse can seem isolating and lonely. Statistics however show differently:

Did you know?

- One hundred percent (100%) of physical abuse begins with emotional abuse and ninety (90%) of the scars left from physical abuse are emotional.

- One in four (1 out of 4) women suffer abuse at some time in their lives.

- A woman is beaten every 15 seconds in the U.S.A.

- Over 3 million women are beaten every year.

- Battering is the single major cause of injury to women in the United States.

- 20% of all hospital emergency room visits by women are attributed to wife beating.

- 4,000 women die each year as a result of beatings; making it more than auto accidents, muggings, rapes and strangers combined.

- 50% of female *deaths* are committed by the man who said "until death do us part."

- 75% of all female related-homicides from domestic violence happen after a woman leaves the relationship.

You don't think it will happen to you?

- Violent families are found in every income category, ethnic background, racial group, educational level and profession. Approximately 1/3 of the men counseled for battering are professional men who are well respected in their jobs and their communities. This includes doctors, psychologists, lawyers, ministers, police and business executives.

- Between 30% - 50% of female high school students report having already experienced teen dating violence.

You don't think it is a problem?

- Between 1.5 to 3 million children witness Domestic Violence annually.

- 600,000 children are physically, emotionally and sexually abused in violent homes a year.

- In 60% of violent homes where the female partner is beaten, so are the children.

- More children are served in women's shelters than woman.

- 70% of all batterers grew-up in violent homes. Boys who were raised in violent homes are more likely to become abusive partners as adults.

- 60% of men 18 - 22 incarcerated for homicide are convicted of killing their mother's batterers.

The above statistics are gathered from the F.B.I., The United Nations and National Abuse Hotline reports.

29

The Many Faces of Abuse

At first impression, abuse appears to be a world of chaos and confusion. However according to the National Domestic Violence Hotline, there are five types of abuse, nine techniques abusers use to debilitate their victims, and one identifiable cycle.

TYPES OF ABUSE

Webster's Dictionary defines abuse as, "The misuse according to the original purpose." Therefore, when any part of our being is *used outside of its original purpose*, we are in a sense, exposed to abuse.

#1: Physical Abuse:

Physical Abuse is any behavior that is designed to control and conquer another human being through the use of physical assaults. Forms of physical abuse include pushing, shoving, slapping, pinching, punching, kicking, unwanted sexual advances (a.k.a. Sexual Abuse/Rape) and any other type of physical violation.

In the United States, physical abuse is one of the primary causes of injury to women. It is classified as a felony and can result in jail or prison time.

#2: Verbal Abuse:

The purpose of words is to communicate and edify. When words are *misused* through name calling, verbal assaults, blaming, shaming, sexual harassing, berating, belittling, criticizing, screaming, sarcasm, and humiliation; or if words are used to control, demean, verbally threaten, or "guilt trip" a person, it is identified as Verbal Abuse.

With Verbal Abuse, the old saying "Sticks and stones can break my bones, but words will never harm me", is not true. Verbal Abuse can and will cause the final blows that will break a person's self-esteem.

#3: Financial Abuse:

Financial Abuse is when finances, which were developed to create exchange, become a tool of control. There are three types of Financial Abuse:

1. Withholding: Withholding is a form of Financial Abuse where one partner withholds finances from the other, leaving the other partner unable to provide for their basic needs.

2. Abusive Spending: Abusive spending is when one partner spends all the income without consulting or discussing the spending (or the outcome of the spending) with the other partner.

3. Burdening: Burdening is when one partner in the relationship refuses to work; continuously finds excuses why they cannot work; or is not able to keep a job or income, thereby placing the entire financial burden on one partner in the relationship.

#4: Spiritual Abuse:

Our spirit being is our tool to connect with God, Spirit or Higher Power.

Spiritual Abuse happens when one partner uses the Bible, God or other forms of religion to control or manipulate another person into submission. In Spiritually Abusive relationships the rules of the religion are always slanted to the benefit of the abuser and to disable and disempower the victim.

#5: Emotional / Mental Abuse:

Emotional Abuse (also referred to as Mental or Psychological Abuse) happens when a person uses emotional techniques to control, coerce, manipulate or intimidate a person into submission. (See Chapter 30 for details).

Emotional Abuse leaves no physical evidence; meaning no bruises or broken bones. However, according to abuse expert Beverly Ingel, M.F.C.C and author of the book **The Emotionally Abused Woman** (Random House Publishing Group, 1992) she states that "One hundred percent of all physical abuse begins with emotional abuse, and ninety percent of the scars left from a physically abusive relationship are emotional."

As quoted by Beverly Ingel, *"Emotional abuse is like brainwashing, in that it systematically wears away at the victim's self-confidence, sense of self-worth, trust in her perception, and self-concept.*

Whether it is done by constant berating and belittling, by intimidation, or under the guise of "guidance" or "teaching," the results are similar. Eventually, the recipient of the abuse loses all sense of self and remnants of personal value.

Emotional abuse cuts to the very core of a person, creating scars that may be far deeper and more lasting than physical ones.

In fact, a great proportion of the damage caused by physical or sexual abuse is emotional.

With emotional abuse, the insults, the insinuations, the criticism and the accusations slowly eat away the victim's self-esteem until she is incapable of judging the situation realistically. She has become so beaten down emotionally that she blames herself for the abuse, and as her self-esteem is then so low, she then clings to her abuser."

THE NINE TECHNIQUES OF ABUSE

Abuse is a tactical process where the abuser uses specific techniques to gain control over their victims. There are nine identified techniques of abuse.

#1: DOMINATION:

Domination is a technique where the abuser uses threats of abandonment, rejection, harm, or loss whenever the abuse victim makes a "choice" *not* approved by their abuser.

The goal of Domination is two-fold: 1) To undermine the victim's confidence, so they doubt their decision-making skills.
2) To train the abuse victim to "ask for permission" from the abuser before making choices.

Domination is the reward/punishment system where the "right" choice results in praise, attention, and affection; and the "wrong" choice brings punishment or abuse.

Living in Domination will make the victim of abuse feel they are losing control of their life; which over time, they will.

#2: ABUSIVE EXPECTATIONS:

Abusive Expectations are unreasonable demands placed on the abuse victim. Examples of Abusive Expectations include:

a. Having to give undivided attention or time to the abuser.
b. Having to find only joy in the abuser.
c. Frequent demands for sex, or the exact opposite, being denied sex.
d. Being expected to put aside everything to satisfy the abuser's needs.
e. Unrealistic lifestyle rules (for example, keeping the house hospital clean or department store organized; not being allowed to gain weight or have any body issues that the abuser finds unacceptable.)

Living in Abusive Expectation creates internal self-doubt in the abuse victim, leaving her asking, "Am I good enough, smart enough, quick enough" as well as other self-doubting statements.

#3: CONSTANT CRITICISM:

Constant Criticism is a) when someone finds constant fault in the victim, and b) when the victim is blamed for all that goes *wrong* in the relationship.

The goal of Constant Criticism is to undermine the victim's confidence, so they feel unqualified to manage their personal life.

#4: EMOTIONAL BLACKMAIL:

Emotional Blackmail is when the abuser threatens the victim with harm, pain or loss if the victim does not comply with the abuser's requests or demands. It is similar to hostage keeping, but rather than the abuse victim being kept physically hostage, they are instead held emotional hostage by the threats of harm or loss. Examples of Emotional Blackmail include:

a. Threats to end the relationship if the abuser does not get his/her needs met.

b. "Distancing", which is a form of withdrawal of attention or affection used to punish the victim until the abuser is given what he or she wants.

c. Harm or destruction to the abuse victim's financial or physical well-being.

d. Harm to the victim's reputation if he or she does not comply with the requests or demands of the abuser.

e. Harm to them self, including threats of suicide if the victim does not agree to the abuser's threats, pleads or requests.

The goal of Emotional Blackmail is to make the victim feel extreme guilt (which is a form of punishment) for thinking of their needs.

#5 UNPREDICTABLE RESPONSES:

Unpredictable Responses are when an abuser uses drastic mood swings, sudden emotional outburst, or inconsistent responses for no apparent reason.

In a relationship with Unpredictable Responses, the abuser creates a constant lack of consistency. For example, one day the abuser will say, "You look great in that outfit." However, the next day the same outfit will provoke a punishment such as, "Why the Hell are you wearing that!"

The goal of Unpredictable Responses is to make the abuse victim live on-edge as well as live in fear of making wrong choices. This then, creates a platform of total control for the abuser as it allows him or her to make rules within the relationship that suits their needs, only.

#6: CHARACTER ASSASSINATION

Character Assassination is when the abuser "assassinates" the character of the abuse victim. Examples of Character Assassination include:

a. An exaggeration of mistakes.
b. Gossiping about their partner's past failures and mistakes.
c. Lying to friends, family and co-workers about the abuse victim, especially if the couple is split.
d. Humiliating, criticizing or discounting the achievements of the victim.
e. Making fun or "joking" about the victim.

The goal of Character Assassination is to discredit the abuse victim's character so that they will lose connection to any support outside the relationship.

#7: GAS LIGHTING / A.K.A. CRAZY-MAKING:

Often referred to as "Crazy Making", the technique of Gas Lighting is used to make the abuse victim feel crazy.

Gas Lighting is when someone continues to doubt another person's perception, memory, or their very sanity.

"Crazy Making" happens when the abuser denies that certain events occurred, or that they made certain statements. The goal of Gas Lighting is to make the victim of abuse feel "crazy" and doubt their personal reality.

#8: CONSTANT CHAOS:

Just as it sounds, a relationship with Constant Chaos is when the abuser creates continual upheavals of chaos. The goal of the Constant Chaos technique is to train the abuse victim to focus only on the abuser. Constant chaos examples include:

a) Unnecessary arguments over "nothing."
b) Sudden illnesses, accidents, and traumas that happen if attention or priority is shown to other people or situation.
c) Deliberate arguments and conflicts to keep the center of attention on the abuser.
d) The inability to enjoy harmony and peace, and as such creates constant disruptions.
e) Negative moods that govern the environment of the relationship.

Living with Constant Chaos can make a victim lose control of their life. *A successful life requires personal attention.* However, a relationship continuously dictated or derailed by Constant Chaos makes it impossible for the abuse victim to focus on anything but the abuser (the chaos or the crises); thereby leaving no time for the victim to focus on their own needs and responsibilities.

#9: SEXUAL HARASSMENT

Sexual harassment is when a person approaches the abuse victim with unwelcome sexual advances, including unwanted sexual comments, written documents of explicit sex, or any sexual act where the victim says "no." Sexual abuse, more often than not, has nothing to do with sex. It instead has to do with control.

30

The Control Factor

Abuse appears to be a condition motivated by cruelty; however, the authentic motivation of abuse is *control*.

As the MANALIVE List of Controlling Behaviors states, *"The purpose of controlling behavior is to destroy a partner by depriving her of commonly held resources that are essential to her well-being and sense of integrity."* Examples of controlling behaviors include:

Controlling Time:

In an abusive relationship, the abuser controls the time of their victim by a) not being on time for appointments; b) committing to do something yet leaving the victim waiting with no response. Or by c) never sharing their plans.

Grandstanding:

Grandstanding happens when the abuser monopolizes conversations by not giving the victim their fair opportunity to speak. Grandstanding can occur in both, public and private environments.

An abuser will Grandstand by talking over their victim or by answering questions for the victim. Or they will Grandstand by monopolizing the conversation when the victim tries to express hers concerns about the relationship. The goal of Grandstanding is to silence the victim from having a voice.

Controlling Space:

An abuser will control space by taking over shared space, or by intruding into the personal space of the abuse victim. Examples of Controlling Space include:

a. Controlling social space by putting limits on friendships and activities; by screening calls; or by prohibiting people to visit the home.

b. Controlling intellectual space by constantly interrupting or arguing with the victim until she gives in to exhaustion.

c. Invading quiet time by talking when the victim wants to be alone or needs silence; especially when she needs to gather her thoughts.

d. Invading privacy by demanding social activities details, past relationship details, opening emails, insisting on passcodes and reading phone texts.

e. Invading sleep by interrupting sleep time with either selfish acts of needs, insisting the victim (only) service the children, or by waking the victim when they feel the need for her to be awake.

f. Controlling personal space by monitoring or controlling the use of the bathroom (for example being required to leave the door open when using the facility); by monitoring the status of their closet or other personal space; or by on-going pressures to have sex when you are not ready.

Material/Financial Resources:

Material Resource Control takes place when the abuser withholds information or items required to maintain a personal existence or well-being.

Body Language and Gestures:

Body Language and Gesture Control happens when the abuser uses body language (also known as *non-verbals*) instead of words to control their victim. Controlling gestures include:

a. sulking
b. refusing to talk
c. withdrawal of affection
d. strutting and posturing
e. stomping out
f. walking away
g. hitting something
h. kicking something
i. driving recklessly

Defining Reality:

An abuser will control their victim by defining their reality by denying certain events happened; by discounting the victim's feelings; or by accusing the victim of trying to start a fight.

Examples of Reality Defining include:

a. Reality Warping ("I know I said it, but it is not true.")
b. Demanding agreement ("What I say is how it is going to be.")
c. Defining the truth ("You don't know what you are talking about." Or "That is not how you feel.")

Defining Motivations:

An abuser will control their victim by telling her *why* she has done what she has done (as though he knows). This is known as Crazy-making behavior which is any behavior that leaves the victim feeling off-balance and confused.

Responsibility Assigning:

An abuser will control their victim by telling her she is responsible for his behavior. It is done to avoid accountability. Examples of Responsibility Assigning included statements such as:

a. "I did it because of you."
b. "I did it because of what happened."
c. "I said it because you made me mad."
d. "I said it because of what happened."
e. "You make me want to ___ you."
f. "What's that _____ doing there?"
g. "How did this happen?"

Assigning Status:

An abuser controls by Assigning Status through puts downs, put ups, sentencing, categorizing and characterizing. Examples include:

a. Put downs: "You are the worst mother." Or "You are a lousy driver."

b. Put ups: "You are the expert at changing diapers."

c. Sentencing: "You are wrong/right to..."

d. Categorizing: "Women are all the same."

e. Characterizing: "You are just like your mother."

31

The Cycle of Abuse

The Cycle of Abuse is a set of patterns and behaviors that identify an abusive relationship. It was originally established in 1979 by Leonore E. Walker as a four-part cycle, but modern day experts have narrowed it to three distinct stages:

Phase One - "The Honeymoon Stage":

The Honeymoon Stage is both the start and stop points in the Cycle of Abuse. At this point of the cycle, the relationship has reached a point of "calm."

The Honeymoon Stage takes place after an altercation has occurred, yet before a new cycle of violence has begun. Following these *intentional* acts of kindness, the relationship will slip into a "honeymoon" period where both parties want to believe the abuse is over for good.

During the Honeymoon Stage, the abuse victim is in a state of emotional shock. Her emotional shock leads to her denial, in which her denial leads to "the non-realistic calm."

On the flip side, during the Honeymoon Stage of the cycle, the abuser will start the process again by "Love Bombing" the victim with kind words, actions, apologies, romance attempts and promises of change and repair.

The Honeymoon Stage has no specific timing, but it lasts until the abuse victim releases her guard and trusts in the "peace" again.

Phase Two - "The Tension Building Stage":

The second phase of the Cycle of Abuse is the Tension Building or "Egg-shell" walking phase.

The Tension Building Phase happens once the abuser realizes the guard of the victim is down, and he (or she) no longer needs to "win" back their partner.

During this phase of the cycle, the abuser's mounting anger will begin to "leak." Meaning he or she will become more edgy and short tempered and little-by-little, verbal or physical "jabs" as well as warning looks and glares replace normal communications. The goal of the Tension Building period is to put the abuse victim "on notice" that the abuser is not happy.

In this stage of the cycle, the victim of abuse begins to feel the pressure and tension in the relationship, as well as, the mounting rejection and judgment. Additionally, the victim will also feel more depressed or anxious in light of the signals of the impending abuse.

As the Tension Building Phase continues to percolate the abuse victim will respond in one of two ways. She will either a) go into a people-pleasing overdrive mode in hopes that her intentional acts of kindness will circumvent the pending abuse, OR b) she will push the situation to an explosive state to execute the abuse.

Many times in light of the latter response, the victim often blames herself for the altercation, as she believes she pushed the situation to the point of explosion. This, however, could not be further from the truth. In reality, she pushed the situation to maintain limited control as to *when* the assault would happen.

Phase Three - "The Abuse Phase":

In phase three of the Abuse Cycle, the acts of violence occur; including physical, emotional and verbal attacks.

Following the emotional or physical assault, the victim is once again in a physical and/or psychological state of shock and goes into what I call the Post Abuse Cycle of Despair.

The PACD includes a migration of emotion that begin at daze and often ends in physical illness. The Post Abuse Cycle of Abuse migrates as follows:

Post Abuse Cycle of Despair
Daze -> Anxiety -> Depression / Despair -> Anger -> Physical illness.

The time frame between, the emotional migration can be as short as a few hours, to a few days leaving the victim questioning her mental stability.

In spite of her despair, initially following the altercation, the abuser will discount or underestimate his actions. He will do this by attempting to convince the victim it was her fault. If, however, the abuser fears the victim might leave, he begins his "Love Bombing" technique to make her stay.

The focus of phase three is to make the victim take responsibility for the abuser's well-being, responsibility for the relationship stability, and to convince the victim of abuse to not abandon the relationship.

During this last phase of the cycle both abuser and victim have a sense of relief that "it" is over and welcome the "Honeymoon" period of reprieve; only to have the cycle start over again.

The timing between the Abuse Cycle can vary from daily, once or twice a year, or just on occasion. As such, many women make the mistake of discounting the cycle of abuse and thereby not deal with the problem directly.

32

What if You Are Being Abused?

(about the W.I.N. Foundation)

If you find yourself or someone you love in an abusive relationship, here are some immediate steps of available help.

Police or Shelter: If your life or the lives of your children are in danger, immediately seek police help, followed by assistance from a local domestic violence shelter in your area. To contact the police within the United States, call 911. To contact a shelter in your area, contact the National Abuse Hotline at 1.800.799.7233.

Counseling: If the situation is not immediately life threatening, contact a local counseling clinic that specializes in abuse recovery. You can find help with a local therapist or with pastoral care at your church or synagogue. One-to-one services may have a required fee. Free counseling services are also available at many shelters.

Support Groups: Group support and connection is a vital element to healing. Local outreaches in your area can provide support and connection. See MeetUp.com (this is not an endorsement), or the community section of your local newspaper. Your local police department, hospital or shelter will also have information on small group support.

On Line Support: If you choose to heal in the privacy of your home, contact my outreach, The W.I.N. Foundation®. Both walk-in classes and an on-line community of healing and empowerment are available. We are located on line at www.WINFoundationInternational.org. or www.DrTracy.tv

We offer a 20-session Healing and Rmpowerment course called "Reclaiming Me" (The Journey from Trauma to Self-Love).

Most importantly, if you find yourself living in abuse remember you are not alone. Get help immediately. Abuse is one of the worst kept secrets, but it is not a secret worth keeping.

MEMO FROM NORMAL LAND®

"Abuse is not a secret we should keep."

Dr. Tracy

Dr. Tracy is an author, speaker, and *"Inspirationalist"* whose slogan is, "Self-Love is Non-Negotiable."

Dr. Tracy began her work in the empowerment industry over twenty years ago with the release of her first book, *The Courage to Say, "No More!"* Shortly following she launched The W.I.N. Foundation®, an international non-profit outreach that specializes in abuse and self-esteem recovery. She created a 20-step recovery program called *Reclaiming Me (The Journey to Self-Love)* that has been taught in over 40 countries, and translated into three languages.

Dr. Tracy's other work includes her books *Breaking Up with A.N.X.I.E.T.Y. (11 Steps to Relief); Real Life Questions and Answer about Abuse*; and *Empowerment is S.E.X.Y. (The four steps to Healthy Selfish)*. She has also created over 30 programs of Empowerment for women available online or at her conferences and workshops.

Dr. Tracy has a Ph.D. in Philosophy, is an abuse recovery expert and a former Mrs. Globe (the Miss Universe for married women). She resides in California and Greece with her family.

For more on Dr. Tracy visit her website at
www.DrTracy.tv

Dr. Tracy

Made in the USA
Middletown, DE
03 March 2019